Stallion Road
A Screenplay by William Faulkner

Faulkner:

A Comprehensive Guide to the Brodsky Collection
VOLUME I: **The Biobibliography**
VOLUME II: **The Letters**
VOLUME III: **The De Gaulle Story**
VOLUME IV: **Battle Cry**
VOLUME V: **Manuscripts and Documents**
Country Lawyer and Other Stories for the Screen
by William Faulkner

Stallion Road
A *Screenplay*

by
WILLIAM FAULKNER

Edited by
Louis Daniel Brodsky
and
Robert W. Hamblin

UNIVERSITY PRESS OF MISSISSIPPI
JACKSON/LONDON

CENTER FOR THE STUDY OF SOUTHERN CULTURE SERIES

Library of Congress Cataloging-in-Publication Data

Faulkner, William, 1897–1962.
    Stallion road : a screenplay / by William Faulkner ; edited by
Louis Daniel Brodsky and Robert W. Hamblin.
        p.   cm.
    "This book is published as a supplement to Faulkner, a
comprehensive guide to the Brodsky Collection"—T.p. verso.
    Adaptation of: Stallion road / Stephen Longstreet.
    ISBN 0-87805-371-9
    I. Brodsky, Louis Daniel.   II. Hamblin, Robert W.
III. Longstreet, Stephen, 1907–   Stallion road.   IV. Faulkner, a
comprehensive guide to the Brodsky Collection.   V. Title.
PN1997.3.F38   1989
812'.52—dc20
                                                          89-16668
                                                            CIP

Contents

Acknowledgments

The editors are extremely grateful to Turner Entertainment Co. for permission to publish Faulkner's screenplay of *Stallion Road*. We especially want to thank Roger L. Mayer, president, and Diana R. Brown, of the legal department, for their indispensable assistance and support.

Stephen Longstreet not only graciously consented to the interview that appears in this volume but also provided useful information and encouragement at various stages of the project. Leith Adams, archivist of the Warner Bros. Collection housed at the University of Southern California, and Harold L. Miller, reference archivist for the State Historical Society of Wisconsin, kindly responded to inquiries and supplied photocopies of relevant materials from the film collections of their respective institutions. We express our sincere appreciation to each of these individuals.

We also gratefully acknowledge the financial support for this project provided by Saul and Charlotte Brodsky of St. Louis and by the Grants and Research Funding Committee of Southeast Missouri State University.

The text of Faulkner's screenplay printed herein is transcribed, with only minor alterations to correct obvious typographical and grammatical errors, from the copy of the script in the Brodsky Collection, now a part of the permanent research holdings of Southeast Missouri State University. Numerous individuals at Southeast have been very supportive and helpful, most notably Bill W. Stacy, Leslie H. Cochran, James K. Zink, Sheila Caskey, and Ginger McCloud. To these friends and colleagues we offer a special thanks.

The preface to this volume includes brief quotations from Stephen Longstreet's *Stallion Road* (Julian Messner, 1945) and Joseph Blotner's *Faulkner: A Biography* (Random House, 1977). We are grateful to the publishers for permission to quote from these works.

Introduction

I

The years 1942–1945 represent the apex of William Faulkner's on-again, off-again association with Hollywood. He had been involved with several film ventures in the 1930s, including two that were quite successful, the adaptation of his own story "Turn About" as *Today We Live* in 1933 and his collaboration with Joel Sayre on *The Road to Glory* in 1936. During that decade, however, Faulkner was essentially an apprentice scriptwriter, feeling his way, learning a new craft, and depending largely upon more experienced filmmakers and scenarists such as Howard Hawks and Sayre for whatever success he achieved. In the 1950s, when Faulkner returned to screenwriting to work briefly on *The Left Hand of God* (1951) and *Land of the Pharaohs* (1953–1954), his heart was not in the work: he was doing it principally out of loyalty to Hawks—and, of course, for the money. However, at Warner Bros. during the 1940s, his most ambitious and productive years in Hollywood, Faulkner developed and matured into a scriptwriter of considerable merit, proving himself to be not merely a competent but actually an accomplished scenarist.

His early work at Warner Bros., best represented by two unproduced screenplays, *The De Gaulle Story* (1942) and *Battle Cry* (1943), was generated by a desire (both his and Hollywood's) to produce propaganda movies in support of the Allied forces in World War II. This phase of Faulkner's Warner Bros. tenure culminated in his successful collaboration with Jules Furthman on *To Have and Have Not* (1944), the rather loose adaptation of Ernest Hemingway's novel that became, in Faulkner and Furthman's handling, another vehicle to express the pro-Gaullist, anti-Vichy sentiments of *The De Gaulle Story* and *Battle Cry*.

But not all of Faulkner's work at Warner Bros. was devoted to patriotic efforts on behalf of the Allied cause. In *Country Lawyer*

(1943), a highly original story treatment suggested by Bellamy Partridge's novel of the same title, Faulkner chronicled the love-hate relationships across three generations of the Partridge and Hoyt families—a treatment that today could quite possibly be developed into a successful television miniseries. With *The Big Sleep* (1944), which he scripted with Leigh Brackett, Faulkner coauthored a script that was translated by Humphrey Bogart and Lauren Bacall, under the direction of Howard Hawks, into a movie that has come to be recognized as a classic. And, though neither of them was subsequently used to produce the film versions of the respective works, he drafted excellent screen adaptations of James M. Cain's *Mildred Pierce* (1944) and Stephen Longstreet's *Stallion Road* (1945). This latter screenplay, the last script that Faulkner completed for Warner Bros. before walking out on his contract and returning to Oxford in September 1945, represents one of his finest Hollywood achievements and clearly demonstrates the extent to which he had finally mastered the peculiar techniques and demands of writing for the screen.

II

Faulkner began work on *Stallion Road* on June 7, 1945, having returned to Hollywood from Oxford following a six-month leave from the studio. He replaced Alan LeMay, who in three weeks on the project had produced only three pages of notes and a nondescript twenty-seven-page treatment. On June 16 Faulkner submitted to the Story Department his own seventeen-page treatment of the story; by July 28 he had completed a screenplay of 134 pages; and on September 1 he turned in the final section of a revised screenplay numbering 151 pages. For reasons that will be discussed below, and despite the impressive quality of the work, Faulkner's script was rejected by the studio. Ultimately, after the joint efforts of writer Emmet Lavery and producer Alex Gottlieb had also failed to provide an acceptable screenplay, Longstreet was called in to script his own novel. It was Longstreet's version that was filmed and released in April 1947, with Ronald Reagan, Alexis Smith, Zachary Scott, and Peggy Knudsen playing the leading roles. Faulkner's version was consigned to the studio vault, where it remained, unread except by a few privileged individuals, until Warner Bros. began disposing of its Faulkner file in the late '70s. Faulkner's script was subsequently acquired in 1982 by Louis Daniel Brodsky for his personal Faulkner collection, and its appearance in this volume marks its first publication.

III

To gain a full appreciation of Faulkner's *Stallion Road,* one must compare it to the original novel by Longstreet. The novel, published in 1945, is primarily the story of the growth and development of Henry Purcell, the narrator. Modeled in large measure upon his creator Longstreet, Purcell is a writer, an Easterner who has come to California to write for the movies while he continues his work as a novelist. Sophisticated, well-educated, and well-versed in literature, art, and music, Purcell meets Larry Hanrahan, a young rancher and veterinarian, and accepts his invitation to visit his Stallion Road ranch in the Sierra Madre region near the central California coast. The visit turns into an extended stay of several months as Purcell, between novels and with time on his hands, becomes more and more intrigued with Hanrahan, the other ranchers, the horses, the range country itself—and especially Fleece Teller, the beautiful young owner of a neighboring ranch who, like Larry, is struggling to revive the region's horsebreeding tradition.

In the course of his extended visit to Stallion Road, Purcell accompanies Larry on camping trips and veterinary calls; participates in area horse shows; becomes a friend and confidant of Larry's sister Rose; has a casual affair with a packing-house girl, Lana Rock; watches Larry become ensnared in an adulterous affair with Daisy Otis, the wife of a wealthy banker; competes with Larry and Richmond Mallard, a roadhouse proprietor, for the love of Fleece; and very nearly loses his life when he, Larry, and others are trapped in a terrible snowstorm. Purcell also observes and admires Larry's scientific experiments devoted to finding a cure for anthrax, and he witnesses Larry's refusal to accept Major Gillray's invitation to abandon the range country and his veterinary practice to devote full-time to his research on behalf of the U.S. Army. At the end of the novel Purcell stands by helplessly as Larry dies from the anthrax he has accidentally contracted during his experiments. By that time, however, Purcell has developed a genuine affection for Larry's range country, its people, and its values, and he concludes that he will stay on the range even after his friend's death.

IV

As even this cursory view of Longstreet's plot suggests, Faulkner found much with which he could identify in this novel. The love of horses and horse shows, a preference for the country over the city, a skepticism about modern ideas of "progress," a respect for simple, ordinary people, a celebration of individual over collective values, the notion that success should be defined in terms of personal satisfaction rather than material reward—all of these sentiments (as reflected in "Knight's Gambit," "The Bear," "Delta Autumn," "Tomorrow," "The Tall Men," and other works of this period) Faulkner shared with Longstreet. Such affinities undoubtedly contributed not only to Faulkner's initial interest in *Stallion Road* but also to the success he was able to achieve in scripting the novel. Faulkner's compatibility with Longstreet's themes appears to have made it easier for him to grasp, from the very beginning, a clear sense of direction and thus minimized the need for extensive revision as the screenplay evolved. Nevertheless, the demands of scriptwriting being quite distinct from those of writing novels, Faulkner was compelled to make significant alterations in Longstreet's handling of plot and characterization. The expertise with which Faulkner effected these changes registers how far he had come in mastering the craft of screenwriting.

V

As would understandably be the case in converting any 300-page novel into a movie script of seventy-five minutes, Faulkner's overriding challenge was the necessity for compression. He solved this problem in part by eliminating many of the individual scenes in Longstreet's novel: for example, the horse frolic in the ocean and the rabbit hunt (scenes that are actually quite powerful in the slower-paced novel) proved to be altogether unnecessary in the love story that became the essential focus of Faulkner's script. Even when he retained Longstreet's scenes, Faulkner frequently dovetailed two or more actions into one. Thus the life-threatening snowstorm and Larry's infection with anthrax, actions separated by several weeks in Longstreet's novel, are merged in Faulkner's script.

Faulkner likewise altered or eliminated a number of Longstreet's characters. For instance, Faulkner's characterization of Hanrahan is quite unlike Longstreet's. Whereas Longstreet's Hanrahan is presented as essentially an irresponsible and divided individual who is still groping for personal identity and direction at the time of his death, Faulkner's character discovers his sense of purpose and social responsibility. In Faulkner's version Larry is portrayed as heroic: he saves his ranch from bankruptcy, prevents a full-scale epidemic of anthrax, earns the respect of the neighboring ranchers, survives a near-fatal infection, and makes a genuine commitment of love and marriage to Fleece. Although this scenario may appear to embody little more than the standard 1940s' formula for the obligatory "happy ending," in actuality Faulkner's characterization of Hanrahan is psychologically complex and sensitive to the nuances of emotional development.

Longstreet's focal character, Henry Purcell, as well as such minor personages as Rose Hanrahan, Lana Rock, and Grandfather Teller, are dropped in Faulkner's retelling of the story. The case of Purcell is particularly revealing, since Faulkner first included the character in the 134-page screenplay but then deleted the character from the final version, reassigning most of his lines to Pelon. This removal of Purcell not only served the interest of economy by eliminating the need for a major actor to fill the role but also allowed Faulkner to place Hanrahan at the center of the action. What is a novel about two principal characters and their multiple and complex love/sex relationships becomes, in Faulkner's more concentrated version, the story of Larry Hanrahan and the two women who compete for his love.

Another significant variation in Faulkner's screenplay is the absence of the thematic preachments that are so prevalent in Longstreet's novel. A case in point is the following speech by Longstreet's Hanrahan: "The trouble with progress, Henry, is that for every toy they give you, they take away some needed hardship. Chasing those horses through the sea is hard work, but it's good for you. Burning up your food inside you is good for you—better than dieting and drinking the blood of oranges. Reading a lying newspaper or listening to a fool howl on the radio may be better than nothing, but making your own life, your own kind of history the way you want it . . . ." Although he had demonstrated in his World War II scripts that he could write propaganda when the situation (and the studio) called for it, Faulkner wisely eliminated such passages from his script of *Stallion Road*, allowing the action to communicate the message through implication and indirection.

However, as impressive as his adaptation of Longstreet's material may be, Faulkner's rich imagination would not allow him simply to edit Longstreet's novel, retaining selected elements and deleting others. A considerable portion of his script is original Faulkner. Certain of these details, such as having Larry live rather than die, seem to be concessions to the expectations of the audiences of the day. Other elements, though, like the trenchant dialogue, the emphasis on a double love triangle (Larry-Mallard-Fleece; Daisy-Fleece-Larry), and the strong sexual content of the script, reflect Faulkner's desire to expand Hollywood's rigidly defined format for movies of this period. The climactic action in which Daisy, in a rage of vindictive jealousy, attempts to murder Larry and then destroys herself by crashing the car over a cliff is altogether Faulkner's invention. Perhaps his most extraordinary accomplishment in this screenplay is the manner in which, through the dynamic interaction of the various characters, he adds dimension to even the secondary roles. Mallard, proprietor of a roadhouse, is a gambler and ladies' man but is also a person capable of a surprising degree of compassion and understanding in his behavior toward the other characters. Pelon rises above the stock figure of ranchhand to become Larry's father-confessor and judge. Dud exhibits a childlike innocence as well as a precocious awareness of the adult situations.

VI

Given the overall quality of Faulkner's screenplay, the obvious question concerns why the studio chose to set aside his script and assign the project to other writers. The answer to that question is undoubtedly complicated and may relate as much to Faulkner's deteriorating relationship with Warner Bros. as to any other factor. Faulkner's growing disenchantment with his long-term contract (which still had four years remaining) and his comparatively low salary had come to a head during the time he was working on *Stallion Road*. In mid-August 1945 he wrote to his agent Harold Ober: ". . . I think I have had about all of Hollywood I can stand. I feel bad, depressed, dreadful sense of wasting time, I imagine most of the symptoms of some kind of blow-up or collapse. I may be able to come back later, but I think I will finish this present job and return home. Feeling as I do, I am actually becoming afraid to stay here much longer." By September 8 Faulkner had definitely made up his mind to leave. On that date Finlay McDermid, head of the Story Department, informed Steve Trilling, a studio executive, that Faulkner had refused to sign papers temporarily suspending, and thereby extending, his contract obligations. McDermid concluded his interoffice memorandum by stating: "It is my feeling that Bill will retire to his native haunts, come what may, unless we can hold out a more tempting bid to him than his present deal offers."

Apparently McDermid's superiors had reached the same conclusion. On the same day that McDermid wrote the memo to Trilling, Emmet Lavery submitted to the Story Department an eight-page outline of his proposed alternate script of *Stallion Road*. This concurrence of events suggests that Faulkner's work may have been shelved in part because the studio by this time recognized, and reluctantly accepted, the fact that he would not be available to make further revisions on the script.

A more plausible explanation, however, is suggested by a letter, dated August 14, 1945, from Joseph I. Breen, Director of the Production Code Administration of the Motion Picture Producers and Distributors of America, to Warner. Breen reported that his group had reviewed Faulkner's initial draft of the screenplay and had concluded "that the basic story seems to meet the requirements of the Production Code." However, Breen went on to explain, there are certain features of the script that need to be toned down. For one thing, all of the scenes involving animals must conform to the standards of the American Humane Society. Citing one passage as an example, Breen noted, "In these scenes of Larry treating the sick sheep we suggest masking all actual scenes of injection." Another concern, undoubtedly a more serious one, related to the adulterous affair between Larry and Daisy Otis. Breen advised, "Kindly keep down to a minimum all scenes of kissing or embracing between Mrs. Otis and Larry." Regarding this latter point, there is evidence that Faulkner, too, was at least partly conscious of the strict sexual standards that would be applied to the script by moralistic and legalistic censors. In the section of his seventeen-page story treatment describing the sleeping arrangements of the characters who are trapped in the snowstorm, Faulkner notes: "Fleece has now moved in her sleep over to Larry; they now lie in each other's arms, Hays [Act] permitting."

Despite Breen's expression of concern, though, Faulkner did not abridge the sexual elements of the story. In his final draft of the script Daisy is still the aggressive, uninhibited nymphomaniac, and she and

Larry continue to flaunt their adulterous relationship in public. In addition, Daisy and Fleece engage in a relentless, often bitter, and sometimes prurient repartee of sexual innuendoes and double-entendres. It was primarily these aspects of the plot that Stephen Longstreet had in mind when he said that Faulkner's script was "a little strong for then." Most likely, it was the unconventional sexual content that eventually led to the studio's rejection of this version of the screenplay. This idea is further substantiated by the fact that neither the revised screenplay by Lavery nor the film version scripted by Longstreet includes any of the objectionable features contained in Faulkner's script.

VII

The ultimate significance of Faulkner's *Stallion Road* is that the script evidences his skillful mastery of the conventions of scriptwriting while at the same time it manifests his compulsion to incorporate, at least to a degree, the subject matter, characterization, and language of realistic fiction. Regarding this latter point, Longstreet's assessment of Faulkner's adaptation seems especially relevant: "I thought it was a magnificent thing, wild, wonderful, mad. Utterly impossible to be made into the trite movie of the period. Bill had kept little but the names and some of the situations of my novel and had gone off on a Faulknerian tour of his own despairs, passions and storytelling. Today it could be made as a New Wave film." While it is debatable whether Faulkner's screenplay strictly adheres to the technical definition of a New Wave movie, there can be no question that it represents a bold and innovative departure from the predictable Hollywood product of the 1940s. Ironically, as Longstreet's statement implies, it was precisely Faulkner's successful fusion of cinematic and fictional techniques that undermined and ultimately defeated his efforts on this project. In effect, what *Stallion Road* demonstrates is that, in Hollywood in 1945, Faulkner was considerably ahead of his time.

Robert W. Hamblin
Louis Daniel Brodsky

Glimpses of William Faulkner:
An Interview with
Stephen Longstreet

by
Louis Daniel Brodsky

L D B :   Where, when, and how were you first introduced to William Faulkner?

S L :   The year was 1937. I was living and working in New York as a graphic artist and as a painter. I remember being surprised when Bennett Cerf, the Random House publisher, called me one morning and said he wanted to have lunch with me.

L D B :   Was this call out of the clear blue?

S L :   Well, I'd done a number of dust jackets for books and I thought Bennett wanted another one. We met for lunch at Radio City, and he said, "I want you to write a novel." I said, "I'm not a writer. I've done a little radio, but I just did that for money." He said, "Well, Bob Haas is very excited about you because of your adaptation of 'The Front Page' for radio; he thinks you're one hell of a writer. He said you told him a wonderful story about your grandfather, and he felt it would make a great novel."

L D B :   Robert Haas was one of the three principals of Random House, wasn't he?

S L :   Yes, along with Don Klopfer. Of course, I was flattered Bob had passed that stuff on to Bennett, but I said, "Bennett, I'm not a writer."

That didn't stop him, though. "I like to take on people nobody's ever heard of, like Saroyan, for example, and put them over," he said.

L D B :   Bennett Cerf was a real promoter, wasn't he?

s L :   He wouldn't give up. When we'd finished lunch, he said, "Come to the office with me; let's talk some more." Random House was down on 57th Street. When we got there, he took me down a hall to a little room—it was actually Saxe Commins' office, I later learned—and there, sitting at a typewriter, banging away, was a little man with pepper and salt hair smoking a little pipe, a Dunhill pipe. Bennett said, "I want you to meet William Faulkner, one of our writers."

L D B :   Somehow, I can't imagine Faulkner brooking this intrusion politely.

s L :   Well, Bill just looked up, didn't say anything; he went right back typing. Bennett continued anyway, "This is Stephen Longstreet. He's going to write a novel for us." Bill didn't even lift up his head this time.

L D B :   Did it bother you that you were intruding on Faulkner?

s L :   No, it was Bennett who was rude. But he didn't even realize it. Then he led me to his office and started in again; this time he offered me an advance. I repeated, "Bennett, I'm a graphic artist and a painter." "I'll give you two thousand dollars advance," Bennett said. You have to remember that in 1937 the Depression was still on and two thousand dollars was like twenty or thirty thousand would be today.

L D B :   How could you refuse?

s L :   Oh, I was tempted, but I was scared, too. Me write a book? "I'll think about it," I said to Bennett and went downstairs. As I was standing out front on 57th Street, seeing the two thousand dollars printed all over everything like billboards, a voice behind me said, "Where can a fella get a drink around here?" I turned around and there was Faulkner in that tweed jacket with the leather patches. I said, "I know an Irish bar down on 3rd Avenue."

L D B :   I take it this was his relaxation hour.

s L :   We went to my favorite bar, and Bill ordered bourbon and branch water. He drank it slowly and quietly, which was fine with me because I was still trying to get my thoughts together. After a while, I noticed that he actually drank continuously, steadily, and that when he'd finish, he'd just hold up his glass, and the bartender would come over and refill it. We spent about three hours there.

L D B :   Can you remember the kinds of things you two talked about in that first encounter?

S L: He talked about "likker," "white lightning," and buying it from moonshiners in Mason jars down in Mississippi. He also told me about how he hunted raccoons at night with torches, the breed of dogs they used; he talked about hunting foxes, too.

L D B :   It seems Faulkner always felt most comfortable when keeping his conversations on topics that had little relevance to his immediate circumstances.

S L :   He wouldn't talk about anything literary. But when I told him about my recent offer, he found it amusing. "Bennett wants you to write a book? Well, Bennett's a con man. He's the greatest salesman. I don't think he reads any of the manuscripts. But do it!" I said, "Write a novel?" and Bill said, "Ten words make a sentence; ten sentences make a paragraph; three or four paragraphs make a page; ten pages make a chapter; twenty chapters and you've got a book." I said, "That easy?" "You believe that, and you'd buy the Brooklyn Bridge," Bill said. Anyway, I became a writer for Random House, and I wrote two or three novels. The first one, *Decade,* even became a bestseller.

L D B :   Did you continue to see Faulkner on his trips to New York or did you lose touch with him?

S L: Oh, we'd meet occasionally when he'd come East.

L D B :   The years between 1938 and 1942 were particularly lean ones for Faulkner. He didn't have the money to travel. In fact, by 1941 he was writing to Robert Haas with increasing persistence about getting Random House to advance him money against royalties on forthcoming novels. And he'd begun imploring his New York literary agent, Harold Ober, to sell short stories he'd been furiously turning out to the slicks for immediate pay to help stave off bankruptcy. At one point Faulkner had even cashed in his life insurance policy to keep his family and other dependents in groceries.

S L :   Well, I'd heard from one of the secretaries at Random House, a friend of mine who wrote me, that Bill was broke and drinking and couldn't even earn enough from his stories to keep going.

L D B :   When was that?

S L :   I'd gone out to Hollywood briefly in 1940, then in '41 for an extended period under contract to Warner Bros. as a scriptwriter; they'd bought three of my novels and wanted me to adapt them to the screen. I wrote Bill then, in late spring or early summer of 1941, asking him if he'd want me to have my agent, William Herndon, look for work for him with the studios. He wrote back saying he'd be grateful for anything I might do for him; he'd take anything.

L D B :   And what was the upshot?

S L :   I was helpful, through Herndon's efforts, in bringing Bill out here to California.

L D B :   Helpful or harmful?

S L :   Well, in hindsight, that's hard to say. Obviously, you know the rest of the story, how Bill ended up getting himself involved with two agents at the same time and signing himself to a seven-year contract with Warners' for a pittance.

L D B :   Faulkner arrived in Hollywood on July 27, 1942, and reported for work at Warner Bros. studio in Burbank the same day, believing the assurances he'd received from James Geller, head of the Warner Bros. Story Department and from his new immediate boss, Robert Buckner, director of his first film assignment, *The De Gaulle Story*, that on completing this project, his contract would be rewritten to include less confining terms of commitment and substantial increases of salary.

S L :   Oh, that was astonishing, finding him working there at the studio for $300 a week. Like most of my fellow writers, I was almost ten years younger than Bill. All of us were in awe of him because of his critical acclaim, and we all knew Jack Warner had taken complete advantage of his drinking reputation, had used him. Hell, I was making $2,000 a week at that time.

L D B :   At least you'd been instrumental in helping Faulkner secure steady income.

S L :   I'm not sure whether Bill held that against me or not.

L D B :   It does seem somewhat ironic, doesn't it, that you should have been responsible for helping to bring Faulkner out to Hollywood in 1942 and for bidding him farewell in September of 1945 after he'd just completed his version of your novel, *Stallion Road?*

s l : Curiously coincidental, yes. Ironic, possibly. I never dreamed that that small gesture of assistance I'd made through Herndon would lead to Bill being assigned to work on one of my novels. After all, Bill was the fictionist, remember; I was the painter and graphic artist turned writer.

l d b : Did you get to spend much time with Faulkner during work hours or socially in the evenings and on weekends?

s l : No. Very few of us got to know him in that way. Buzz Bezzerides was an exception. Bill stayed with him for two years, as I recall. But I did get acquainted with him because he and I shared a car pool. It was during the war and Bill would ride. We would pick him up in downtown Hollywood—I think at the time he was staying in the Roosevelt Hotel. I don't know where he went later.

l d b : I believe he stayed at the Highland Hotel some of the time before he took a room in the Bezzerides' house in Santa Monica during his 1944 and 1945 studio stints. Did Faulkner contribute to your conversations back and forth in the car between L.A. and Burbank?

s l : Bill never took part in the discussions . . . not at all. There were five of us—there was Milt Gross, a writer named Val Burton, myself, and I can't remember the other besides Bill. One day, as we got out of the car in front of the studio, Burton turned to me and said, "Faulkner likes you." I asked, "What makes you think so?" He said, "Because he said 'good morning' to you."

l d b : Did you ever actually see Faulkner typing away on a screenplay in the Warner Bros. writers' compound or discuss with him any of his projects?

s l : Bill was extremely serious-minded. When he was in his office he was either writing or drinking, and he wouldn't have wanted to be distracted on either account. But Bill never discussed with me or with anyone else there, to my knowledge, any of the projects assigned to him. However, he did have a reputation for being able to turn out "too much" work. There were times when I would come into his office with my pad and paints. He never seemed to mind me sketching him at work or painting his portrait in watercolors. He'd go right on typing. I don't think he wrote when drunk, but he did type away on a hangover. I painted him in that condition a few times. In fact, the watercolor I sent you, the one showing Bill's drooping eyelids that I painted in 1945 while he was working on the script for *Stallion Road*, was done while Bill was nursing a bad hangover.

L D B :   While you were there at Warner Bros., didn't Faulkner share screen credit for two very strong, successful films, *The Big Sleep* and *To Have and Have Not*, both done under the direction of Howard Hawks?

S L :   Yes, he did. By that time, Faulkner was working with a writer named Jules Furthman, who was Howard Hawks's favorite writer. And Furthman told me, "If you want to be a success in Hollywood, latch onto a director and convince him that every picture he makes will be a disaster unless he uses you." Furthman was a great politician as well as a very good writer. He was teamed with Faulkner on *To Have and Have Not*, a film loosely adapted from Hemingway's novel. Now, whether Furthman used to steal Faulkner's pages or not and submit them as his own I don't know—there was a rumor to that effect, but nobody ever really knew how much Faulkner actually wrote on that script. I have a feeling Bill also felt the same way toward Hawks as Furthman did—that without him, Hawks couldn't succeed. And Hawks, to Bill's credit, did have great faith in Bill. It went both ways.

L D B :   Faulkner collaborated with Leigh Brackett on *The Big Sleep*. It has been difficult to determine just how much each contributed to that script also. Do you remember Leigh Brackett or anything about Faulkner's involvement with that project?

S L :   No, I don't. None of us ever quite knew how much of the actual writing was Faulkner's. By the end of 1944, however, Faulkner's reputation as a screenwriter had grown high among his fellow writers as a result of the success of those two pictures. But Bill was still drinking heavily. I couldn't do a God damn thing with him. Buzz Bezzerides was really Bill's nurse; he took care of him like a baby.

L D B :   Buzz has described to me how Faulkner would suffer incessant bouts with drinking that would incapacitate him to the point of requiring sanitarium care.

S L :   Maybe without Bezzerides Faulkner would have been fired. Bill used people. Like so many drunks, he'd take advantage of you; women out there, too.

L D B : Can you recall any social gatherings you and Faulkner and some of your fellow workers attended?

S L : Bill wouldn't get about socially much; he never went to any of the big parties around town. I do remember once when Jim Geller, the story editor at Warner Bros. who admired Bill very much, had a party, a dinner party attended by Aldous Huxley, Christopher Isherwood, and a lot of Hollywood types and myself and my wife. We insisted that Bill go. He went, but just sat all through dinner not uttering a word while Huxley was telling everything to all of us there—how to make an atom tick, the secret of the Great Pyramids—carrying the entire conversation. Bill would just hold up his glass and the maid would come over and refill it— bourbon and branch water.

L D B : Like he did that first time you met him in that Irish bar on 3rd Avenue in New York City.

S L : Yes, but I'd never seen Bill drink as he did that night—and he was a pretty good drinker, very quiet, very gentlemanly; he never staggered in public. On our way out, my wife asked Bill how he liked the party. He didn't say anything, made no response as though he hadn't heard her question. So she changed her approach slightly, asked instead, "What did you think of Aldous Huxley?"—to which Bill curtly replied, "An educated jackass. A writer should just follow life with a notebook and keep his mouth shut."

L D B : Faulkner certainly wasn't one for small talk unless it revolved around a campfire or occurred over continuously refilled glasses of whiskey in familiar surroundings with people who didn't threaten him.

S L : Bill gave me the impression that he always knew his own worth as an artist and that he didn't have to defend himself or his art to anyone. Actually, he had a rather low opinion of most living American writers. There was a solid, hot case of ego in the guy.

L D B : There were a few writers for whom he had respect, though.

S L : I remember asking him what writers he liked among his contemporaries, and he said, "There are only three of us in America today: Hemingway, myself, and Thomas Wolfe . . . I'm the best!" I said,

"I think Tom Wolfe is a mess." I had known him back in Brooklyn. "I think he's a phoney." Bill said, "No. No. Wolfe, myself, and Hemingway are the three writers."

L D B :   And in that last order you recited. That was how Faulkner would rate them years later when giving interviews. I've read some of Faulkner's transcribed comments from those interviews in which he defended Wolfe, despite his awkwardness, his prolixity, on the basis that of the three, Wolfe took the greatest risks with his art; he showed no cowardice, evidenced "courage" in striving to create an original style, and wasn't afraid to fall on his face for staring up at the stars.

S L :   And that was what Bill said was Hemingway's greatest failure; he wouldn't risk getting beyond what was tried and true for him, wouldn't take chances beyond the macho mask.

L D B :   What other discussions of that nature, if any, did you have with Faulkner?

S L :   One day, Bill was coming into the writers' compound with a magazine containing a long article on the symbolism in his novels, how the novels were all interconnected within the mythical county so that there was a universal thing, while the novels retained their regional quality, and just how remarkable this plan was.

L D B :   I believe you're referring to Malcolm Cowley's article, "William Faulkner Revisited," which appeared in the *Saturday Review of Literature* in April, 1945.

S L :   Yes, Cowley's piece, to become part of his introduction to *The Portable Faulkner*. I remember Bill laughing like hell as he read parts of it to me aloud. "Bill," I said, "you really had no plan for all those novels?" He said, "Damn it, no! I just wrote them as they came to me. Now, of course, some critics see a great plan there, but when I started, I just sat down and wrote them out one at a time."

L D B :   I'm surprised Faulkner would admit this.

S L :   Oh, he'd get a bit oiled on the bourbon in my office. Mostly his responses were always curt or derisive, sardonic. I remember once asking him what his greatest ambition was as a writer. He said, "My great ambition was to write for the *Saturday Evening Post*." He paused and when I didn't respond, remained quizzical, he finished his thought:

"And there's where I had it all over Tom Wolfe. He only sold 'em one story. I musta sold them a dozen."

L D B : How would you size up William Faulkner from your vantage of having known him in the late thirties and a Warner Bros. from 1943 through 1945?

S L : He was a proud, dour little man with a lean, biting sense of humor at times, and when alone, his drinking often went way out of control. He led a rather dull life out here. He bought a mare, loved to ride—I was told he was very poor at it, often was thrown. He could also be a very arrogant man; he wouldn't autograph books for anybody, and at that time people were sending him rare first editions of his books, collectors' items, and he never answered them. He never signed or returned them. You'd walk into his office, and they'd be piled up against the wall, all these rare Faulkners which weren't really so rare in those days.

L D B : Rare, I would say, only in the sense that they were scarce, hard to find even in secondhand bookshops because of their originally low print runs determined by a correspondingly limited reading audience for his fiction. And that, of course, was the reason he was at Warner Bros. augmenting his income to support himself and his extended family in Oxford, Mississippi.

S L : Hate it he might, but Bill worked hard at the studio. He was sincere about his job and was one of the few writers I knew who wasn't destroyed by Hollywood. Most novelists who came to stay out here sold out whether they wanted to or not. But Bill separated his life into compartments so that a screenplay was a screenplay. Although he had no great love for the medium or for his scriptwriting, he did the best he could.

L D B : With regard to Hollywood, there are two prevalent conceptions or misconceptions that students of Faulkner seem to cling to: first, that he had contempt for California, its lifestyles, its raison d'être, if you will, and secondly, that he held the medium itself and his own competency within the medium in extremely low regard. I believe that Faulkner made his feelings quite clear on the former subject, but that he remained ambivalent, and at times was even ambiguously outspoken concerning the latter two-headed issue. What do you feel about this?

S L : Sure, there's no doubt that Bill hated California and the claims it made for Art—most producers collected modern art and fancied themselves among the chosen patrons of culture. Bill's comment to me was, "Artistically, Southern California is the plastic asshole of the world." When his contract was coming up for renewal, I wondered if he would stay on. I knew he would be leaving when one day—it was a bright, wonderful, sunny day—we were standing at the studio gate waiting for our car pool, looking up at the mountains all in fine color and making a perfect composition, and Bill scowled, "What a god damn place! One leaf falls in one of those god damn canyons, and they tell you it's winter." The next week Bill was gone.

L D B :   How do you relate to the commonly accepted attitude that Faulkner was never more than a mediocre screenwriter?

S L :   Well, Bill was better than most of the overpaid hacks. There's no real literature here, just craftsmen, wordmongers, gag writers. Bill worked very hard at being a scriptwriter, and by the time he left Hollywood in September, 1945, he had become capable of writing with the best of his lot, the few real talents who were here then.

L D B :   His last major project at Warner Bros., writing a story treatment and completing his own revised screenplay for *Stallion Road*, which he did between June and September of 1945, would seem to bear out your judgment—for me, at least, this screenplay not only is very creative and technically sound, but actually approximates good literature. Mr. Longstreet, you once told an interviewer that you felt Faulkner's script "was a magnificent thing, wild, wonderful, mad" and that "today it could be made as a *New Wave* film." Do you still feel that way?

S L: I sure do! Bill wrote a brilliant screenplay of *Stallion Road*, and I thought it was great, too. It was a little strong for then. It was quite powerful, didn't pay too much attention to my novel. What Bill had done was to write a purely Faulknerian narrative, a beaut, all shadow and highlights and with the smell of the best horses.

L D B :   Shouldn't the fact that it was rejected by the studio and that ultimately you were called in to adapt your own novel for the screen be taken as a condemnation of Faulkner's screenplay?

S L :   Not at all! I think it was simply too good to be made into the trite movie of the period the studio and its audiences demanded.

L D B :   I feel privileged to finally make Faulkner's screenplay of *Stallion Road* available to the public. How do you feel about this prospect?

S L :   I'm pleased you're publishing Bill's unique screenplay. Maybe because I wrote the novel and the final version of the screenplay for the film, I feel even more privileged—privileged that Bill Faulkner gave us his own conception of my original creation.

Stallion Road
A Screenplay

by
WILLIAM FAULKNER

From a Novel
by
Stephen Longstreet

Cast of Characters

LARRY HANRAHAN A young veterinary interested in the scientific problems of his profession, he has recently returned from overseas service. Moody, personable, he affects disinterest in . . .

FLEECE TELLER Who loves horses as much as does Larry. Young and beautiful, she is doing her best to make a success of her nearby ranch.

DAISY OTIS As attractive as hell—and she knows it. When Larry went off to war she married Ben Otis, a man with money. But she has a roving eye and body.

RICK MALLARD Attractive, smooth, he operates a pleasant roadhouse popular with the horsy set.

MAJOR GILLRAY An Army officer interested in Larry's anthrax experiments.

GUS LINDSTROM A fine, sincere rancher who acts as spokesman for the smaller ranchers in the Valley.

PELON Larry's Mexican man-of-all-work.

DUD TELLER Fleece's kid brother.

OLD MIKE An old groom who helps Fleece run the ranch. He is an old family standby who takes the place of the father which Fleece and Dud don't have.

PEDRO Fleece's stableboy.

FADE IN

EXT. COUNTRY ROAD   NEAR ENTRANCE TO STALLION ROAD RANCH
NIGHT

Dud Teller enters, galloping, bareback on a tough western pony. He is about ten, in overalls. He is in a hurry. He has been riding hard for a good distance. The pony is almost spent. He reaches the gate to the ranch. Over it is a sign:

STALLION ROAD RANCH
Laurence Hanrahan

Dud gallops through the gate and goes on toward the house.

EXT. STALLION ROAD RANCH HOUSE   NIGHT

Dud gallops up to the house and flings himself off before the horse has stopped.

The house is low, ranch-house type. It is dark. In background is a long stable, a single dim light burns in it.

Dud drops the reins of the panting horse and starts running toward the house when he sees the light in the stable, turns without stopping and runs toward it.

INT. STABLE   HALLWAY

Dud runs in. The light comes from beyond a door to one side. The stable is lined with stalls containing horses. Dud runs toward the door where the light is, shoves it open and enters.

INT. TACK-ROOM   (LAMPLIT)

It contains the usual saddles on trees, bridles and harness on pegs, etc. But it also contains a bench cluttered with microscopes, test

3

tubes, ovens, etc., showing how the room has been converted into a sort of makeshift laboratory. There is a cot against one wall.

AT COT

A man is asleep beneath the tumbled not too clean blankets, his head covered and only his feet exposed. Dud rushes over, snatches the covers off his face. The man is Pelon, a Mexican, about 40. He is Larry's hostler-stable-foreman. In the light, we now see Dud's anxious worried face. Pelon awakes.

> DUD   *(anxious)* Where's Doc?

> PELON   Where would any honest man be this time of night? In bed asleep.

Before he has finished speaking, Dud whirls to dart out. Pelon reaches out his arm and catches him.

> DUD   *(struggling)* Lemme go! I got to get Doc! Our mare Sultana's sick, maybe dying.

> PELON   *(holding him)* Sultana? Why didn't you say so in the first place? Larry's down at Mallard's. *(starts to get up, still holding Dud)* I'll telephone him.

> DUD   *(struggling)* Durn telephoning! Don't you know the horse show's day after tomorrow?

> PELON   *(holding him)* But the All-Western show for mares is a month off yet. That will give even me time to telephone in—

But Dud breaks free, runs out, Pelon lies down again.

> PELON   *(about to recover his head with the blanket)* Eh, little man. Maybe a sick mare can get him away from that wheel, but I doubt it.

He covers his head again.

DISSOLVE TO:

EXT. MALLARD'S TAVERN   NIGHT

Dud gallops up on the spent pony, flings himself down again and runs toward the door.

INT. MALLARD'S TAVERN   BAR

Dud, just entered, is struggling in the grip of a big bruiser of a bouncer, who grasps him by the collar.

DUD (*struggling*) Lemme go, you ape! I got to get in! My mare's sick.

BOUNCER We got plenty of half horses here, and some of them are mares too. But they ain't eating no hay. Outside.

He picks Dud up, struggling, flailing at him with his fists, and thrusts him outside.

EXT. TAVERN   NEAR ENTRANCE DOOR

The bouncer is facing Dud, who is almost crying now with impotent rage and anxiety.

DUD I got to come in, I tell you! Our mare's dying!

BOUNCER Then gwan home and hold her head—

Dud lowers his head and rushes at the bouncer, who grasps him again and holds him off while Dud flails vainly at him with his fists.

BOUNCER Stop it, stop it, you little wildcat—

Dud, seeing he is getting nowhere, jerks free, runs out. The bouncer looks after him. Then he turns toward the door. As he does so, a missile of some sort (grapefruit rind perhaps), flung by Dud, strikes him on the back of the head. He turns angrily, in time to see Dud dart around the corner of the house. The bouncer starts to follow, gets an idea, pauses, turns and enters the door rapidly.

EXT. REAR OF TAVERN

Dud enters, running, looks about until he locates a door, obviously a rear entrance, runs to it, jerks it open, reacts.

IN DOORWAY   TO REAR ENTRANCE

The bouncer is standing in the door, hands on his hips, looking down at Dud.

BOUNCER Maybe it's your ears and you can't hear good. Or maybe you ain't got no home—

The bouncer makes a motion at him. Dud darts away again. The bouncer withdraws and closes the door.

INT. KITCHEN

The bouncer is just closing the door. A tremendous fat chef is stirring something on the stove; dishwasher in background; a helper passing food through slot to waiters, etc.

DISHWASHER   *(as bouncer passes)* What's the matter?

BOUNCER   Nothing. Just a kid.

DISHWASHER   Why don't you let him in?

BOUNCER   *(approaches stove, sniffing)* Sure. And have the whole range sayin' we're runnin' a kindergarden. *(to chef, sniffing as he leans over the pot)* What you got there? Smells like Rick might have bought you a cookbook at last.

DISHWASHER   *(over shoulder)* Except who would have taught him to read it?

EXT. REAR OF TAVERN   DUD

—is now actually crying with rage, anxiety and the necessity for haste. He is baffled, is bent on getting in, does not know how he will do it. A vague idea strikes him. He begins to empty his pockets of the things which a small boy might carry, hoping to find something to help him, producing a broken knife, a few marbles, a slingshot, a wad of string, a mashed melted candy-bar; then with a dawning expression he takes from a forgotten pocket a shotgun shell. His idea is complete, his face lights with grim determination. He moves rapidly now, back to the kitchen wall where the kitchen flue projects, drags a barrel up beneath it, finds a box, sets it on top of the barrel, climbs precariously up, reaches up and drops the shotgun shell down the flue, jumps down, runs to the kitchen door and stands crouching beside it a moment. A muffled explosion sounds from inside.

INT. KITCHEN

The shell has just exploded inside the stove. The pot has overturned. Still bending over the stove, the bouncer and the cook look at each other slowly, too surprised to move yet. Their faces are completely blackened, like two blackface minstrels. The dishwasher, slack-jawed, his head turned. After a second he recovers, leaps toward the door.

DISHWASHER   Lemme out of here!

BOUNCER   *(grimly; he knows who is to blame though he doesn't know just how)* Yeah, me too.

He shoves the dishwasher aside, goes quickly to the door, grasps the knob in grim, determined anticipation, and jerks the door open. But before he can pass through it, Dud darts in. The bouncer grasps at him, Dud wriggles free like an eel, darts across the kitchen toward the pantry door.

BOUNCER   *(whirls)* Catch him!

He lunges for Dud again, grasps him. They plunge into a table and overturn it (whatever further comedy we can get), the furious cook joining in the chase of Dud who is as hard to hold as a cat as he tries to get through the pantry door, until the door opens and Rick Mallard enters.

Mallard is about 40, well dressed in dinner coat, a gambler and innkeeper of the better sort.

MALLARD   *(as he looks at his ruined kitchen, and at the three people sprawled before him)* What the—? *(he recognizes Dud)* What's this? a stick-up, or am I just being protected?

ANOTHER ANGLE   MALLARD, DUD, BOUNCER

MALLARD   *(to Dud)* What's wrong? Is your sister—?

DUD   Naw. It's Sultana. She's dying. I was trying to find Doc, but this ape wouldn't let me in—

BOUNCER   And so he tries to blow himself in by droppin' a stick of dynamite down the stovepipe.

DUD   It wasn't nothin' but a shotgun shell, you big yellow reformatory ape. *(tries to pass Mallard)* Get out of the way; I got to find Doc—

BOUNCER   *(starts angrily)* Is that so!

MALLARD *(to bouncer)* Hold it. *(to Dud)* If you want Larry, come on.

He turns toward the pantry door, shoving Dud along before him.

BOUNCER Oh, he wants Larry Hanrahan, huh? Why didn't he say so?

Mallard doesn't answer. He is about to push Dud through the pantry door, when the bouncer raises his voice.

BOUNCER Tell Larry I'll take his dame home, huh?

MALLARD *(turns)* Sure. Then her husband can drive you back.

Mallard and Dud exit.

INT. GAMBLING ROOM   AT WHEEL

The wheel is crowded with players. In the center are Larry Hanrahan and Daisy Otis, playing.

Larry is about 30, has an out-of-doors face, has just finished Army service as a horse expert. He wears loose, worn, comfortable ranch clothes: worn riding pants perhaps, a worn, easy tweed jacket, etc.

Daisy is in her 20's, looks wealthy, smart clothes, much jewelry. She is a wife not for love but for money, married to a wealthy banker. Her principal occupation is nympholepsy; she now has a yen for Larry, since he is the newest man she knows.

She has a big stack of chips, Larry a much smaller one. The wheel has stopped, bets are paid off and raked in. Larry waits until Daisy makes her bet. Then he bets directly against her, as if by deliberate intention. Daisy watches him, shows displeasure, as Larry withdraws his hand. The croupier picks up the ball.

DAISY *(to Larry)* There's still time to change it.

Larry says nothing, calm, inscrutable. The wheel spins. Daisy wins. Larry loses.

DAISY *(stacking her winnings; low voice)* Why don't you follow my bets?

LARRY *(calmly)* I don't take money from women.

DAISY Not even from me?

LARRY You mean from your husband, don't you?

DAISY *(viciously)* Oh, a purist! What you mean is, money is the one thing you don't take from women.

LARRY *(waiting for her to make her next bet)* I wouldn't know— not until I've been tempted.

Daisy is angry. With an angry movement she makes another bet. Calmly, Larry again bets against her choice. The wheel spins again. Mallard enters behind them.

MALLARD Larry—

Larry doesn't answer, watching the wheel. Mallard touches his shoulder. Larry glances back.

MALLARD You've got a patient.

LARRY Sorry. My office closes with a time lock at sunset.

He turns back to the wheel. It slows, stops. Daisy wins. Larry loses again.

MALLARD *(to Daisy)* Excuse me, Mrs. Otis.

He shoves in between Daisy and Larry. Daisy looks up, recognizes him, watches as Mallard puts his hand over the rest of Larry's chips.

DAISY *(to Mallard)* That's right, Rick. Don't let him play anymore. Even you should be tired of winning his money now.

MALLARD *(to Daisy)* I just want to speak to him a minute. *(to croupier)* Watch Doctor Hanrahan's stack. *(to Larry)* It'll only take a minute.

LARRY *(to Daisy, as he turns)* Maybe you better quit too, without me to show you what you ought not to do.

DAISY *(gives him a look)* Maybe that's what I want.

MED. CLOSE   MALLARD AND LARRY

—as they come up to Dud.

MALLARD *(to Larry)* It's Fleece Teller's Arab mare—*(interrupts* *himself, indicates Dud)* This is her brother Dud. They bought the old Thompson ranch about four years ago, after you went into the cavalry.

DUD   *(interrupts)* It's Sultana. She's down in the stall. Fleece says you got to come—

LARRY   Why didn't she call Doc Halliday? He's closer than I am.

MALLARD   Sure. Halliday can give the mare a shot of gin. That's what he does his practice with nowadays. Come on, Larry. Miss Teller's having a pretty tough time of it—nobody to help her run the place but an old groom and this kid—

LARRY   *(watches Mallard)* I thought it was a sick mare that needed me.

Mallard says nothing; they watch one another.

LARRY   Which is it? Am I going because of a sick horse, or because of Miss What's-her-name?

MALLARD   Teller. Fleece Teller.

LARRY   Well? Which?

MALLARD   *(after a moment)* All right. If you're not going, say so. Then I can try Halliday.

LARRY   So you can try Halliday? I thought it was the kid needed a vet.

Mallard says nothing, Larry watching him. After a moment he turns to Dud.

LARRY   Okay, Bud. Hold it a minute.

He goes back to the wheel.

AT WHEEL   LARRY AND DAISY   MALLARD BEHIND THEM

LARRY   *(to Daisy)* I've got to go see a sick mare. Rick'll send you home—

DAISY   *(viciously)* I heard that much too. I just didn't hear which one you're going to see.

LARRY   Which what I'm going to see?

DAISY   Which mare?

CROUPIER   Make your bets.

LARRY   *(hand on stack; to Daisy)* What are you waiting for?

DAISY   I've quit.

LARRY   Maybe that's what I need, too.

He sets out his whole stack, the wheel spins, stops. He loses.

DAISY   *(drily)* Was it?

LARRY   *(turning away)* Goodnight.

Daisy doesn't answer. Larry moves away.

ANOTHER ANGLE   LARRY, DUD, MALLARD

LARRY   *(to Dud)* Come on, kid.

MALLARD   Thanks, Larry. Leave his pony here. I'll send it home. Tomorrow.

LARRY   *(over shoulder, pushing Dud on)* I'll tell Miss Teller to thank you.

He and Dud exit.

                                                    WIPE TO:

EXT. TAVERN

Larry and Dud approach Larry's parked station wagon. It shows hard service. Lettered on the door is:

LAURENCE HANRAHAN
Veterinary
Sierra, California
R.F.D.

Larry opens the door. Dud gets into station wagon. Larry is about to follow, when Daisy runs out of the inn. She stops.

DAISY   Larry.

Larry pauses, turns his head. Daisy has stopped, is waiting. After a moment Larry turns and goes back to her.

LARRY AND DAISY   AT ENTRANCE TO TAVERN

DAISY   You didn't tell me goodnight.

LARRY   Didn't I? Goodnight.

DAISY   Not that way.

He doesn't move, he doesn't even seem to know what she means. She raises her face to be kissed.

LARRY   *(after a moment; still playing dumb)* Oh, I see.

He bends and touches her lips, very platonic, not touching her otherwise.

DAISY   Not that way either.

LARRY   Recess is over. I'm back at work now.

DAISY   What a fool you are. Maybe it's because you haven't been home long enough to know your clientele. Fleece Teller is supposed to be Rick Mallard's.

LARRY   Yeah? Who supposes it?

DAISY   Rick, for one.

LARRY   Maybe he's right. Rick's a good guy. And I'm going to see a horse.

DAISY   *(quite cold and grim)* Maybe you'd better stick to that. Goodnight.

Larry doesn't move, looking at her.

DAISY   Why don't you go, then?

LARRY   I am.

He takes her in his arms. She makes no response. He tilts her face, kisses her, draws her close, beginning to hold her hard. She puts one arm around his neck, responds to kiss, her other hand fumbles a wad of something from her coat pocket, thrusts it into his pocket. He feels the movement, breaks, takes out the object: it is a wad of banknotes, money.

DAISY I won it; not my husband.

LARRY But you won't have it long, carrying it around loose in your hand.

He takes her purse from her, opens it, puts the money inside, closes the bag and hands it back to her.

DAISY I can't even buy you, can I?

LARRY I don't know. *(he strikes the bag lightly with his fingertips)* You haven't tried very hard yet. *(he starts away)* Goodnight.

He goes on. Angle widens to include Mallard watching near the station wagon, though neither of them has seen him yet. Daisy watches Larry.

DAISY Be sure it's the horse.

LARRY *(walking)* I'll try to. But you know me: if there's one thing I can't resist, it's temptation.

He goes on to the station wagon. Daisy turns and enters the house. As Larry reaches the wagon, he sees Mallard, stops.

LARRY Don't tell me I'm stepping on your toes there too.

MALLARD Not there. And not even with Miss Teller, at this rate.

LARRY They tell me that can't be done at any rate.

MALLARD I'll risk it though, if you'll just get on and see about that mare.

LARRY Oh yes, that's the Sultana mare who might be pretty good for the All-Western next month. I've got a mare for that, too.

MALLARD But I don't believe you're going to win it this way.

Larry opens door to station wagon, in which Dud already sits.

LARRY Thanks for the good opinion anyway. *(he gets in)* I'll tell them you'll send the pony home tomorrow?

MALLARD   Right.

He steps back as Larry drives away.

DISSOLVE TO:

EXT. TELLER RANCH   NIGHT

House in background as Larry drives up. It has a struggling look about it, as if there were not much money here, that the people who now own it have courage and independence but not much else, which is the fact. As Larry's lights swing across the front of it, they pick up Fleece Teller, waiting at the edge of the drive with a flashlight. She wears faded levis and a man's shirt, is pretty and, at the moment, seething with anxiety which has now taken the form of anger. The car stops, Dud jumps out, Larry follows.

EXT. DRIVEWAY   TELLER'S RANCH   DUD, LARRY, FLEECE

DUD   Here's Doc. I had to go all the way to Mallard's joint to get him. But Rick made him come.

Fleece is seething, but her face is so calm that Larry doesn't get it yet. Neither he nor Dud knows she is talking to him for a moment.

FLEECE   I see. That's why it took you so long. Only, I wouldn't say I was behind the game and it took me a few hours to get back even; I'd say my sense of honor as a gentleman wouldn't let me quit while I was ahead.

LARRY   (*gets it now*) Okay. My sense of honor wouldn't let me quit. I think I heard you had a sick horse here.

FLEECE   (*turns*) This way.

When her back is turned, Dud mimics a cat toward it, says in undertone, for Larry's benefit as well as his own satisfaction: "Meow." But Fleece turns and catches him before he can recover.

FLEECE   (*to Dud*) And you go to the house.

DUD   After I done spent half the night getting the doctor?

FLEECE   Yes. You may have to spend all tomorrow getting the doctor back home by way of Mallard's gambling room.

She waits while Dud retreats. Then she starts to turn, stops, whirls again on Larry.

FLEECE   What did you say?

LARRY   Nothing. I'm just being glad your mare isn't as sick as somebody told your brother she was.

FLEECE   What do you mean?

LARRY   Apparently you didn't need a doctor: you just wanted somebody to vent your temper on.

FLEECE   *(after a moment)* Sorry. *(turns; quieter)* Come on.

Larry follows.

INT. STABLE   A STALL

Larry and Fleece stand over the mare, which is lying down in the stall. The mare is a fine Arabian. Larry kneels as he examines the mare rapidly and skillfully, seems to go straight to the trouble, prods the mare lightly about belly with fingertips.

FLEECE   Will she die?

LARRY   Yes—if she stays lying down long enough.

FLEECE   Then do something—don't squat there looking at her!

LARRY   Okay. Give me a halter.

FLEECE   *(puzzled)* A halter?

After a second she turns, takes a halter down from a hook beside the door, hands it to Larry.

FLEECE   What are you going to do?

Larry doesn't answer. He slips the halter on the mare, petting and caressing her, talking to her, in a joking, soothing voice.

LARRY   *(to mare)* So. You're quitting, huh? Want to live private for a while; lie up in bed and have your meals on a tray, huh? *(he rises, hands the halter-rope to Fleece)* When I give you the word, lift her head. *(he steps around behind the mare, taking off his wide hat)* Go on. Haul her head up. Stay clear of her feet.

FLEECE   No! I won't do it. She's my horse—

LARRY   Go on. Jerk her head up. What do you think she is—glass?

Fleece raises the mare's head; as she does so, Larry strikes the mare across the hips and hind legs with his hat—more noise than anything else—shouting as he strikes the mare again and again.

LARRY   *(shouting to mare)* Hup! Hup with you. Hoy! Hoy!

The mare surges up on her forefeet. Larry strikes her harder, shouting, sets his shoulder against her flanks and almost raises her by main strength until she stands at last, trembling.

LARRY   There you are. Sure she would have died—lying there on her left side for another day or two, with nobody around here to make her get up. What do you use here for grooms, anyway?

FLEECE   *(furious sarcasm)* Very well, *Doctor.* Now what?

LARRY   She's got colic, that's all. Bad feeding. I suppose the same groom does the feeding too.

FLEECE   *(humbly almost, but asking no favors, making no excuses, proud still, facing him)* I do the feeding.

LARRY   *(his voice, manner change completely; voice quiet, impersonal)* All she needs is a drenching. She'll be all right tomorrow. If you have an empty quart bottle and some warm water—

FLEECE   *(quietly, turns)* Yes.

She exits. Larry looks after her. As though without knowing he is doing it, he stands stroking the mare's neck. He gives the idea that he might be stroking Fleece's hair. When Fleece is gone, he seems to recover, realize what he is doing, that he was actually stroking Fleece's hair, reacts, turns, takes up his bag and begins to open it.

                                                    DISSOLVE TO:

INT. TACK-ROOM

There is a cot in it. It is obvious that Fleece had spent the night here, in anxiety for the mare, waiting for the doctor. A table bearing a portable hot plate and coffee pot, cups, etc.

The door opens. Fleece enters, followed by Larry. An alarm clock on the table says: 3:40. There is a bench bearing ewer, washbasin, a towel. Larry's sleeves are rolled up.

LARRY *(as he enters)* Sure. She's all right. Just be a little more careful about her feed.

Fleece goes to the bench, fills basin, steps aside.

LARRY *(follows)* Thanks.

He begins to wash his hands. Fleece goes to the hot plate, plugs the cord to heat the coffee. Larry dries his hands, rolls down his sleeves while they speak. Fleece has to make an effort to speak. She is honest enough to eat crow when she is wrong, but she is still proud.

FLEECE I want to apologize.

LARRY Okay. We'll call it done.

FLEECE I guess Rick's already told you how it is—

LARRY *(interrupts)* Rick didn't, but plenty of other people did.

FLEECE What do you mean?

LARRY Nothing. Rick's a good guy. But I believe you were saying something about your mare.

FLEECE Yes. As Grandfather would have said, she's the last shot in the Teller locker. If I don't win that, Dud and old Mike and I might be picking beans.

LARRY I see. For the ten thousand dollar All-Western next month.

FLEECE Yes. I suppose you're entering your mare. I've heard of her.

LARRY Maybe.

FLEECE *(her tone friendly now)* I guess you're entering something in the local show here day after tomorrow.

She turns, becomes busy with coffee pot. Larry watches her back.

LARRY *(drily)* Yeah, the Madre Range local, with entrants coming from as far as 20 miles. *(still watching her back)* Are you that broke?

FLEECE *(turns quickly)* Did Rick tell—? So that was why you tore yourself from his wheel. *(she draws from her pants pocket a thin roll of money)* After all, I suppose I am keeping you from your more important affairs, insisting on giving you a cup of coffee. How much do I owe you?

LARRY What for? I thought you were dealing with a roulette player, not a veterinary.

FLEECE Then you'd better take something for another stake in the game. Maybe no other sick horse will interrupt you tonight.

LARRY Okay. Maybe I will take another stake in Rick's game.

Before she can move, or even knows what he is about, he moves lightly and quickly to her, grabs her and kisses her, releases her. She has not moved at all.

LARRY Aren't you even going to sock me?

FLEECE What for? Did I have anything to do with that?

LARRY That's right. You don't like to pay your debts, do you?

Fleece looks at him, cold, inscrutable, deliberately puts her arms around him, kisses him, realizes suddenly when it is too late that the kiss is getting out of hand, jerks free, panting, then suddenly slaps him with all her might across the face, steps back, panting.

LARRY *(after a pause)* See you at the horse show. Goodnight.

Larry exits as Fleece looks after him, completely unsure of her emotions.

FADE OUT.

FADE IN

INSERT: A CLOTH BANNER

—lettered:

MADRE RANGE HORSE SHOW

Camera pulls back to reveal:

EXT. VILLAGE STREET   FULL SHOT   DAY

The banner is stretched across the street. The street is decorated with other banners and placards to the same horse show effect, directions for stabling, registration, etc. The street is crowded, has a festive air. It is locally the big day of the year. The town is crowded with visitors, on foot, mounted, in horse carts, station wagons, cars. Camera moves up to a:

CLOSER SHOT   A TRAILER   (SAME STREET)

—hitched behind a battered small coupe. The trailer contains Fleece Teller's Arab stallion. She and her old groom, Mike, a fatherly-looking man of sixty, are on the ground, altering the check-lines which hold the stallion in the trailer. Fleece is working rapidly and expertly. A truck containing three blanketed horses enters, is about to pass, slows to stop.

ANOTHER ANGLE   TO INCLUDE TRUCK

Larry is driving the truck, Pelon beside him. Between them sits Major Gillray, U.S. Cavalry. Larry leans out.

LARRY   (*to Fleece*) Any trouble?

FLEECE   (*very coldly*) No thank you.

LARRY   Sultana all right this morning?

FLEECE   Wasn't she visited by an expert?

LARRY   See you in the ring, then.

FLEECE   Why not?

Fleece becomes busy again with the lines. Larry shrugs, starts to drive on.

PELON   (*quickly to Fleece*) Good luck to you, Señorita.

Fleece glances up at the new voice, whose intent is obviously kind.

FLEECE   Thanks. I may need a lot of it.

PELON   Perhaps not. You have much horse there.

Larry has stopped the car, waiting for Pelon to get done with these unexpected amenities.

LARRY   (*to Pelon*) You through now?

PELON   *(pulls his head in)* Señor.

Larry drives on. Fleece has already turned back to her work, is still tightening a line when a coach-and-four enters. It is driven by Mallard; beside him are Daisy Otis and a sporty-looking man with a hunting horn, slightly tight. Mallard sees Fleece, pulls up beside the trailer.

COACH-AND-FOUR   BESIDE FLEECE'S TRAILER

As Mallard pulls to a stop, the man with the horn blows a salute on it.

MALLARD   *(to Fleece)* Good morning.

Fleece turns, pleasantly, examines the group on the coach, sees that the man with the horn is already tight.

FLEECE   Good morning. You've started a little early, haven't you?

MALLARD   Just a few of us. You know Mrs. Otis, don't you?

DAISY   *(voice silken)* Yes. I know Miss Teller. I think we're going to know each other much better, too.

FLEECE   Are we?

DAISY   Yes. I hear you had to have a doctor with your mare a few nights ago, darling.

FLEECE   Yes. She's all right now though.

DAISY   What a shame . . .

FLEECE   What do you mean?

DAISY   *(airily)* A veterinary is such a comfort against loneliness—especially at night. You won't have any reason to call him in now.

FLEECE   *(holds her own)* Oh, you mean bait. I've just bought a toy roulette wheel. That's all the bait this doctor seems to need.

MALLARD   Now, girls; now, girls. *(to man with horn)* Give Mrs. Otis and Miss Teller a cocktail. Their throats must be dry.

MAN WITH HORN   *(producing a vacuum bottle)* Right you are, Ben Hur. *(uncaps bottle, starts to pour)*

DAISY   Not for me. Give it all to Miss Teller for a consolation prize.

FLEECE Not for me either. I've won so many consolation prizes lately that my mantel's full.

DAISY Let's go, Rick, if we're going.

Mallard gathers the reins, then he leans down. His heart is really in his eyes: an incongruous thing, with his suave hardness and success.

MALLARD You have lunch with me?

FLEECE Yes.

Mallard gathers the lines to drive on.

MAN WITH HORN Curse the luck.

MALLARD *(checks horses)* What?

MAN WITH HORN I was going to ask Miss Teller to lunch myself. *(to Fleece; he is obviously attracted)* Perhaps, if I could bribe the horses to run away with Rick, or hire a groom to kidnap him—?

FLEECE If you can.

MAN WITH HORN It's a date, then?

FLEECE We'll see.

DAISY *(to man with horn)* Better pour *yourself* a consolation prize, Harry. *(to Mallard)* Let's go, Rick.

MALLARD *(to Fleece)* Till noon, then.

FLEECE Yes.

MAN WITH HORN *(raising his horn)* A salute to all frustrated stags!

DAISY *(as coach starts to move)* Does, too, darling.

The coach moves away.

DISSOLVE TO:

EXT. HORSE-SHOW GROUNDS   DAY

It is a big pasture, transposed for this occasion into a show-grounds, has a "community-homemade" look. Many parked cars, a banner over the entrance:

W E L C O M E
MADRE RANGE HORSE SHOW

Gay crowd, some cosmopolitan, Abercrombie and Fitch horsemen and -women, others, ranchers in ordinary western clothes; temporary marquees, tent-stables, rope-enclosed paddocks and corrals, many horses, trailers, etc., grooms, hostlers, owners. The show ring is temporary, with temporary, contrived grandstand, judges' stand, etc.

SHOT OF SPECTATORS   (CENTERING ON MALLARD, DAISY, MAN WITH HORN)

The man with the horn looks a little soberer now. Mallard is watching the horses in the ring intently, his heart is obviously on Fleece and her success. He is paying no attention to his companions. Daisy is looking at the man with the horn.

    DAISY   *(to man with horn)* I thought they told you not to bring that thing here.

    MAN WITH HORN   They just said don't blow it. It only cheers winners, anyway.

    DAISY   It cheered one loser back in the village this morning though. *(to Mallard, remarking his intentness, needling him)* It's Larry's horse she'll have to beat—if that's what's on your mind. They're on horses, you know, not in bathing suits.

    VOICE FROM LOUDSPEAKER   Let them canter!

    MALLARD   Maybe she won't need a bathing suit—on Sultan.

    DAISY   A horse might help her—some, anyway. But the bathing suit wouldn't hurt.

    MAN WITH HORN   They never do.

    VOICE FROM LOUDSPEAKER   Reverse—and canter!

FULL SHOT   THE RING

—as the horses reverse without breaking stride, canter.

    VOICE FROM LOUDSPEAKER   Bring them to the judges' stand.

CLOSE SHOT   THE HORSES

—as they are brought up and stopped facing the judges. The blue is given to Larry, the red to Fleece, the yellow to a third horse.

TWO SHOT   LARRY AND FLEECE

—mounted.

LARRY   *(to Fleece)* Tough luck.

Fleece doesn't even look at him as she turns her horse away.

FLEECE   Congratulations.

MALLARD, DAISY, MAN WITH HORN   IN CROWD

Mallard shows worry, disappointment.

MAN WITH HORN   *(largely)* After all, it's just a horse show.

DAISY   *(silken, vicious, needling Mallard)* Only there was a cash prize with that blue ribbon.

MAN WITH HORN   Not much, though.

DAISY   It would have paid some of the expense of entering her mare in that ten thousand dollar prize one next month, though. *(needling Mallard)* Of course, she has rich professional men friends to borrow from—but then, only the rich aren't too proud to borrow—

MALLARD   *(moving suddenly)* Will you excuse me? *(he starts quickly out)*

DAISY   *(after him as he exits)* We'll even wish you luck.

AT EXIT FROM RING   FLEECE AND MALLARD

Fleece sitting her stallion, Mallard standing beside her.

MALLARD   Tough luck.

FLEECE   Thanks. At least it was my fault—not Sultan's.

MALLARD   You rode rings around him.

FLEECE   Enough of the right people didn't seem to think so.

MALLARD   To blazes with them. Let's get some lunch.

FLEECE   *(first bitterness shows)* Yes. I won't need to pass judges with a knife and fork in my hands.

She moves the horse on, Mallard follows.

DISSOLVE TO:

INT. RESTAURANT   FULL SHOT   NOON

It is a tent, makeshift, with borrowed or rented tables and chairs, very likely a "Ladies' Aid" sort of thing, set up for the day. The waitresses are all amateurs: Junior League, etc. The profits—what profits there are after they finish paying a week afterward the butcher and baker bills which they had forgotten about—to go to the Community Chest. It is crowded with lunchers, cosmopolitan horsy people and plain ranchers.

Fleece and Mallard are at a table in foreground. Daisy, followed by Gillray, man with horn, and Larry, enters and crosses the room some distance away, not passing near the table.

DAISY   *(calls to Fleece)* Too bad, darling. Maybe it's like gambling; maybe it means you are lucky at love.

MALLARD   *(to Daisy)* We're going to do better this afternoon, though. *(to Larry)* Larry.

Larry approaches the table. Daisy, man with horn, and Gillray go on to where a waitress shows them a table. Larry stops at the table, very cold, interrogative.

AT MALLARD'S TABLE   LARRY, MALLARD, FLEECE

LARRY   Morning, Miss Teller.

Then he turns to Mallard, waiting.

MALLARD   We're going to beat you on the jumping this afternoon.

LARRY   *(polite but perfectly flat)* Miss Teller outrode me this morning. Those judges need glasses.

MALLARD   Let's hope they have them at the All-Western next month. You're entering your mare for that too, I suppose?

LARRY   Yeah. *(he looks at Fleece speculatively; then away,* *quickly)* Gus Lindstrom's got a good horse over bars. Maybe she'd better count on a loan from the bank first.

FLEECE *(quickly)* Don't keep Doctor Hanrahan standing here, Rick. His guests are waiting for him.

LARRY Yeah. *(turning, speaking to no one directly)* Better luck this time.

He goes away. Mallard leans forward, quickly solicitous.

MALLARD I'm sorry. Did I talk too much—?

FLEECE It doesn't matter. Can I have some coffee?

DAISY, MAN WITH HORN, GILLRAY AT THEIR TABLE

—as Larry sits down. The waitress is waiting.

DAISY Was it a sale?

LARRY *(takes menu)* What sale?

DAISY Or maybe she'll just use the look on Rick's roulette wheel.

WAITRESS *(to Larry)* How will you have your beef, Doctor Hanrahan?

LARRY With bread and potatoes.

DISSOLVE TO:

A BARRED JUMP DAY

—as a horse goes over it. A section of spectators can be seen. In the center of them, nearest to the jump, are Daisy Otis, Mallard and man with horn. Mallard is watching with complete fascinated attention. Spectators applaud the jump.

VOICE FROM LOUDSPEAKER Coyote. Owner, Mrs. Major Astor. Professional rider.

Coyote squares away, runs at the jump, takes it. Applause from spectators. But Mallard hardly watches the jump; he is looking out toward where the horses are starting from.

VOICE FROM LOUDSPEAKER Highline. Owner, Gus Lindstrom. Gus Lindstrom, Junior, up.

Highline, the third horse, takes the jump. Applause. Mallard is still looking out.

DAISY *(to Mallard)* Here comes Larry's horse. Now's your chance.

MALLARD Chance for what?

DAISY Scare it. Wave your handkerchief at it when it takes off.

VOICE FROM LOUDSPEAKER Beaustar. Stallion Road stables. Major Gillray, United States Army, up by courtesy of owner.

Beaustar jumps. Major Gillray not only rides well, it is obvious this is a good horse. Much applause. Mallard watches this jump, but quickly looks out again.

VOICE FROM LOUDSPEAKER Sultanito. Teller Ranch. Miss Fleece Teller up.

Sultanito jumps. Applause. This is what Mallard has been waiting for. Attendants run in, raise the bar.

LAP DISSOLVE TO:

THE SAME BARRED JUMP

Attendants raising the bar higher.

VOICE FROM LOUDSPEAKER The bar is now at five feet. Three contestants left—Highline, Gus Lindstrom, owner; Beaustar, Stallion Road Ranch; and Sultanito, owned and ridden by Miss Fleece Teller— Just a moment, please, there seems to be something happening down there—

SHOT OF SPECTATORS

The faces of the spectators all crane as they look out, wondering what is going on.

VOICE FROM LOUDSPEAKER Here it is: Doctor Hanrahan himself is now up on Beaustar, replacing Major Gillray. . . .

LARRY AND GILLRAY   AT BEGINNING OF RUN TOWARD THE JUMP

Larry now on his horse, Gillray below him on the ground.

GILLRAY It's quite all right. You know the horse better; naturally you can get more out of him than a stranger.

LARRY Thanks.

He looks up, sees:

FLEECE   ON HER HORSE

—watching him. She looks quickly away.

VOICE FROM LOUDSPEAKER Another change. Dr. Hanrahan and Mr. Lindstrom have offered Miss Teller the privilege of jumping first, as gentlemen should. Miss Teller has declined. They drew for position and she will jump second. Mr. Lindstrom!

FULL SHOT   THE RING

Gus Lindstrom, Jr., brings his horse out, walks him, reined back and tense, up to the jump, gives him time to gauge it, walks him back to the start, turns and holds him, lets him go.

CLOSE SHOT   THE JUMP

—as Lindstrom, Jr., goes over it. His horse ticks the bar.

WIDER ANGLE   SHOWING SECTION OF SPECTATORS

They are now tense. There is no sound. Man with horn and Mallard, in their old places, Daisy between them, watch anxiously.

VOICE FROM LOUDSPEAKER Miss Teller!

FULL SHOT   RING

Fleece walks her nervous horse up to the jump, holds him, while he gauges it, turns and walks him back to the start, turns him broadside to the jump and holds him again, leaning forward over his neck, patting him, soothing him, holds him until he is ready, leans further forward, settles herself in stirrups, lets him go.

CLOSE SHOT   THE JUMP

Fleece takes the jump clean.

SHOT OF SPECTATORS

Again there is no applause. Mallard reacts, looks quickly and anxiously out of scene toward starting line.

VOICE FROM LOUDSPEAKER Doctor Hanrahan!

CLOSE SHOT   GILLRAY'S FACE

He alone has suspected what Larry intends to do.

FULL SHOT   RING

Larry on his horse as he walks the horse to the jump, halts him a moment as the others had done, walks him back to the starting line, turns him and puts him at the jump without any pause, skillfully contriving to make the horse take the wrong lead and so throwing himself offstride, doing it so cleverly that nobody but Gillray realizes what he has done at first.

CLOSE SHOT   THE JUMP

The horse runs at the jump and makes a gallant effort despite Larry, almost clears the jump, but crashes the bar with a hind foot, knocks the bar down, the worst jump of the three.

SHOT OF SPECTATORS

Crowd applauds.

CLOSE SHOT   FLEECE   AT JUDGES' STAND

—receives the check. Crowd applauding.

LARRY AND GILLRAY

Larry on his horse, Gillray on the ground beside him. Gillray knows what has happened. He does not approve of betraying an honest horse that way.

GILLRAY   (drily) I congratulate you. A little hard on the animal though, isn't it?

LARRY   (noncommittal) Thanks.

GILLRAY   As a habit, it might go a little hard with the rider too, someday.

LARRY   Not with a good animal.

GILLRAY   (strokes the horse) Yes, he's a stout fellow.

LARRY   See you at the car.

GILLRAY   Right.

Larry rides on.

HIGH-BARRED GATE TO A CORRAL   A GROOM

—standing beside it. The gate is a little better than five feet. Sound of hooves running OVER. The groom looks out, shows alarm, ducks suddenly aside as Larry's horse runs in, jumps the gate clean.

FLEECE

—as she watches Larry jump the gate. This proves what she has suspected. Her face is grim. She is holding the folded check in her hand. She tears it into pieces across and across, walks out.

INT. LARRY'S TENT-STABLE

Fleece enters, walking fast. Her face is grim, furious, cold. As she enters, Larry emerges from the rear shadows. They pause. Then still cold and grim, Fleece strides to him, flings the torn scraps of the check into his face, turns and strides out.

DISSOLVE TO:

HORSE-SHOW GROUNDS   TWILIGHT

The horse show is over. The tents and marquees are empty, some are being taken down, along with the rope corrals. The parked cars are starting up, crowds dispersing, cars drawing trailers containing horses pass through the gate beneath the banner.

SHOT OF MALLARD'S COACH

It is standing in the middle of the road, blocking the procession, so that the other vehicles have to turn out to pass it. They are annoyed. On the coach sits only the man with the horn. He has passed out now, is asleep, the horn in his arms.

LARRY'S STATION WAGON   A SMART CONVERTIBLE BESIDE IT

Daisy and Larry, waiting for someone. Daisy is impatient.

DAISY   Leave that rattletrap of yours for him, let him come out by himself.

LARRY   He doesn't know the way.

DAISY He's a cavalry officer: he can certainly find it, with all his West Point training. Come on.

She goes to the convertible. He follows. They get in.

DAISY You're some horseman, aren't you? Some jumper. Kiss me. Then maybe I won't tell what I know.

LARRY Your blackmail's no good now.

DAISY But this is. Try it. *(giving him the business)* You black-guard, that would doublecross a poor horse—

He kisses her. After a while, still kissing, he reaches out his hand, fumbles, finds the switch key and turns it on. Still kissing him, Daisy reaches out her hand and turns the switch off again.

INT. FLEECE'S TENT-STABLE   MALLARD AND FLEECE

Mallard holds Fleece in his arms. She is crying with rage and impotence. The stable is empty now, horses gone.

FLEECE But to do it that way—just because you told him I needed the money—to insult me, treat me as if I were a child and wouldn't know he deliberately made the horse false-break—

She makes an effort, pulls herself together, tries to free herself. He releases her.

FLEECE Handkerchief, please.

He gives her his handkerchief. She wipes her eyes, recovers.

FLEECE There. All over now. You're a sweet guy, Rick—to be a tough gambler.

MALLARD Only I don't seem to be sweet enough.

FLEECE What do you mean?

MALLARD *(soberly)* Women only cry over the guys they either love or hate.

FLEECE Well, I wasn't crying over you—I was crying on you. And I just said what I'd like to do to Doctor Hanrahan. . . .*Doctor* Hanrahan—

MALLARD *(drily)* Yeah. I heard you.

FLEECE *(after a moment; watches him)* So that's it. Is it being a gambler that's made you an expert in female hearts?

MALLARD Or maybe it was having to be a *tough* gambler made me the expert.

FLEECE *(moves closer)* But don't you think there might be just a little about them you don't know yet?—even a tough gambler? *(moves closer to him, lifting her face)* Just a little, maybe?

He catches on then, takes her in his arms, still diffident as though he were not certain, kisses her, tentatively, then with ardor, withdraws a moment.

MALLARD Dinner, then?

FLEECE Yes.

He kisses her, holds her. Sound of running horse out of scene. They break, look toward the door as her stableboy, Pedro, runs in.

PEDRO *(rapidly)* It's Sultana. She's down again—

MALLARD *(as Fleece starts to run out)* I'll find Larry—he hasn't left the grounds yet—

FLEECE And have him tell me again it's only colic and that I baby her too much? Go to Mrs. Astor's and telephone Dr. Halliday. Tell him to come at once—*(she runs again)*

MALLARD Shall I come with you—?

FLEECE *(running out)* Just call Dr. Halliday.

She exits.

DISSOLVE TO:

INT. LARRY'S STABLE   LARRY, GILLRAY, DAISY, PELON   NIGHT

A row of stalls along the wall, in each of which stands a horse. One stall is open, the horse has been led out. It is old, spavined, bony, sick-looking, a scrub horse to begin with. Gillray is looking at it.

GILLRAY Anthrax? You gave him anthrax two weeks ago? He ought to be dead.

LARRY Yes.

GILLRAY   Then you've found it. You've got a serum.

LARRY   No. Not yet. Sometimes it works and sometimes it doesn't. It's about fifty-fifty yet. I lost two last week.

Gillray glances at the other stalls, over each door of which the head of another old worn-out sick-looking horse looks out.

GILLRAY   But you've got four still alive. That's no fifty-fifty. It's sixty-six percent saved. Well, that's enough for me. We'll take over.

LARRY   I don't believe I get you.

Telephone rings offscene. Larry pauses. Pelon starts to move.

DAISY   *(moves)* I'll go. Even a new sick horse will be a change.

She exits. Pelon watches her. We see he does not like her at all, disapproves of her on Larry's account.

GILLRAY   Why, the army'll take your experiments over—you and your plant both. *(glances about, contemptuous)* Plant? We'll give you a plant—all the money you need—assistants, a thousand horses for your guinea pigs. Then you can quit this piddling around, curing hogs and sheep of colic and mange, give all your time— maybe rid the world of the disease the army and all the other people who use horses have never beaten yet—

LARRY   But the cavalry, the army, first.

GILLRAY   Why not? A man can have a worse boss than Uncle Sam—

LARRY   I think you've overlooked something—

DAISY'S VOICE   *(offscene)* Larry. It's Gus Lindstrom—

LARRY   *(turns)* Excuse me a minute.

As he turns to exit, Pelon suddenly follows him.

AT DOOR   TO TACK-ROOM

Daisy stands in the door as Larry starts to pass her. Pelon has followed him in background.

DAISY   I wonder how I'll like army life. *(Larry, passing her, pauses)* I may like it—a post full of handsome young West Pointers with the dew still fresh on their gold bars . . .

PELON   Perhaps you may not need to learn, Señora.

They react to this, Larry especially. Then he goes on.

LARRY   *(passing her)* So you're going to enlist, are you?

DAISY   I'd say we were being drafted. Wouldn't you, Pelon? Or maybe you're the one who's not going?

INT. TACK-ROOM   LARRY

—as he takes up the phone.

LARRY   *(into phone)* Yeah, Gus?

INT. LINDSTROM RANCH HOUSE   GUS LINDSTROM   AT PHONE

He is a man of 60, a rancher, not too rich.

LINDSTROM   *(into phone)* It's not cholera. I think I know cholera when I see it— Yes, I've segregated them—

INT. TACK-ROOM   LARRY   AT PHONE

LARRY   *(into phone)* Then keep them up. Turn the rest of the flock back onto the range, keep them as far away as possible . . . Yes, I'll come on out.

He puts the phone down.

WIDER ANGLE

—as he crosses to his laboratory table, lifts his bag from underneath, opens the bag, begins to put instruments, phials, etc., into it. Gillray and Pelon in background. Daisy has disappeared.

LARRY   *(packing busily, over his shoulder to Gillray)* Sorry, I've got an 80-mile call to make. It's mostly uphill, so I won't get there until daylight and I probably won't be back until tomorrow night. Seems to be a cholera scare. Pelon will take care of you, or if you must go back to town Mrs. Otis can drive you.

GILLRAY   Thanks. Before you go, what about my proposition? You were saying I had overlooked something.

LARRY   Yes. That this range is my home, these range farmers and ranchers and stock-breeders are my people. If and when I find an anthrax serum they'll have it first. After that, I'll think about your cavalry. Thanks just the same for the offer of the lab and the cushy job.

GILLRAY   You can't be serious.

LARRY   I'm trying to be.

GILLRAY   It's the government, you know. We can draft you.

LARRY   *(pleasantly)* Then you'll probably have my serum.

He continues to pack. At last he takes from a drawer, handling it very carefully, a locked steel box. They watch him.

PELON   So that's it, huh?

GILLRAY   *(quickly, glances from Pelon's face to the box)* What? *(comprehends)* That's your serum. So it's not cholera.

LARRY   I'm afraid not. *(quickly)* But it mustn't get out. You can imagine what would happen on this range if an anthrax scare got started.

LARRY   *(to Pelon, directly)* Do you hear, Pelon?

PELON   I heard you.

LARRY   *(to Pelon)* No word, until I'm certain. Better not tell anybody where I've gone even.

PELON   No one is to know where you have gone even.

LARRY   *(looks about)* Where's—?

Daisy enters. She now wears her coat.

LARRY   *(to Daisy)* Will you drive Major Gillray back to town? I've got to make a call.

DAISY   Pelon will drive him back in your station wagon. *(as they stare at her)* My car's much faster than yours. If you really want to save poor Lindstrom's sheep.

LARRY   I won't get back until tomorrow—maybe not then.

DAISY   All right. My car's used to being out all night.

A take, while they stare at her in indecision.

PELON   *(to Larry, in such a tone that for a moment they don't get it)* You and Señora Otis are alike in one thing, anyway.

LARRY   *(to Pelon)* Yeah?

PELON   You don't seem to have any trouble either forgetting she has a husband.

Larry slaps Pelon, staggers him back. Pelon catches his balance, already poised, his hand poised quickly just above his waist, where we can now see the possible knife. Larry knows it is there, Gillray immediately surmises it.

GILLRAY   *(to Larry)* Look out, Hanrahan!

Larry glances about. There is nothing in reach in case Pelon draws it. Daisy shows combined terror, yet at the same time a glittering pleasure. Slowly Pelon's hand drops.

PELON   *(to Larry)* You have forgotten yourself.

LARRY   *(at Pelon's mercy, still on guard, but giving no ground)* So did you forget you're a servant.

PELON   I have never been a servant here, and you know it. I am here because I know horses—and because I liked you.

LARRY   I know it. I'm sorry. Forget it, will you?

PELON   *(staring at Larry)* I will try.

LARRY   *(suddenly offers his hand)* Here—

PELON   *(not moving)* I said I will try. You'd better get started, if Gus really has anthrax. Señora Otis can drive the Major to town, unless he will stay the night.

LARRY   I thought you were going to try to forget it.

PELON   *(after a moment, shrugs)* Of course.

Larry takes up his bag, pushes Daisy toward the door. Daisy gives Pelon a vicious look, safe now.

DAISY   Yes. Maybe we'd better stop and speak to the sheriff first—

LARRY   *(savagely; shoves her on)* Get on, will you!

They exit. Pelon watches them out.

GILLRAY   *(to Pelon)* If you'll run me in to town—

PELON   *(moves)* Come then, Señor Major.

They exit.

EXT. STALLION ROAD RANCH HOUSE   PELON AND GILLRAY

—beside the station wagon as Daisy's convertible goes down the drive.

PELON   *(as though to himself, looking after the convertible as it speeds away)* She loves him. I was there this afternoon. I don't mean that one, of course.

GILLRAY   The worst misfortune a man could suffer is to be loved by that one. *(curiously, watching Pelon)* Were you really going to draw the knife? You had one, didn't you?

PELON   *(rouses, looks at Gillray, shrugs)* For an instant, yes. But then, a man can't always. . . . *(he stops, watching Gillray)* But after that, you're wondering why I didn't hit him back with my hand.

GILLRAY   Not that. A man will return a blow for the sake of his own pride. But not to make a Roman holiday for a. . . . *(he stops, shrugs too)*

PELON   Thank you, Señor.

He opens the door. Gillray gets into the station wagon. Pelon follows. The wagon drives away.

DISSOLVE TO:

EXT. STALLION ROAD RANCH HOUSE   LATE THAT NIGHT

Sound of running horse, then Dud enters, bareback as before, on the same pony. The house is now dark, but he doesn't hesitate. He rides on toward the stables.

EXT. STABLES

Dud runs the horse in, jerks it up, flings himself down already running toward the tack-room, flings the door open, enters.

INT. TACK-ROOM

Pelon is asleep as before, his head covered, his feet out. This time, without stopping, and before Pelon can wake and move, Dud runs across and snatches the blanket off. Pelon wakes. The clock is at: 4:25 A.M.

DUD   Where is he? Where's Doc? It ain't no colic this time—

PELON   He's gone.

DUD   No, he ain't. I already been to Mallard's—

PELON   No. Mrs. Otis took him off in her car.

DUD   You mean he won't be back tonight?

PELON   You know Mrs. Otis. What do you think?

Dud whirls. When he turns, we see he is crying now.

DUD   *(already running)* Durn Doc Hanrahan! *(he runs out; his voice comes back)* Durn him!

PELON   *(sitting up in blankets)* Sí, little man. I, too.

DISSOLVE TO:

EXT. TELLER RANCH   STABLE   DAWN

Dud rides in on the horse. It is about spent now, as is Dud, worn with fatigue and sleeplessness. He gets down, wearily, but still going as fast as he can, enters the stable.

INT. STABLE   AT SULTANA'S STALL

Sultana lies on the ground. Fleece, Dr. Halliday, a snuffy man of 60, and Mike, the old groom who has served the Tellers many years, stand anxiously over her. Fleece is kneeling. She rises quickly as Dud runs in.

DUD   Doc's gone. He won't be back until tomorrow. They wouldn't even tell me where. So you'll have to go after him yourself and bring him back.

FLEECE   *(bitterly)* So he does intend to win that prize. Well, I'm not surprised.

DUD   You got to go! You got to!

FLEECE   Why? Any man who would false-break a good horse at a jump certainly wouldn't hesitate to let a mare die for ten thousand dollars.

MIKE   *(to Fleece)* You can bring him back. Find him and apologize.

FLEECE   Apologize? For what?

MIKE   Pedro told me what happened to that check you won.

DUD   *(as Fleece stares at Mike; defiantly)* You can find him! He just went off with Mrs. Otis, that's all. All you need to do is find her car—

FLEECE   *(quickly)* With Mrs. Otis? Then I certainly won't interrupt them—

She turns quickly toward the door.

MIKE   *(moving too)* That's right. You get your coat. I'll get the car out.

FLEECE   *(hurrying out)* But don't think it's on her account! I want a doctor for Sultana, and I'm going to have one.

MIKE   *(following)* Sure. I'll get the car.

He and Fleece exit. Halliday sits down in a chair against the wall, closes his eyes; he is old and tired. Dud looks down at the mare.

MED. CLOSE SHOT   DUD AND SULTANA

Dud kneels beside the mare's head, caressing her, murmuring to her.

DUD   That's right. Tha-a-t's right. You just lay still and rest. Fleece is going to get Doc Hanrahan, and he'll—

He pauses, motionless, an idea has struck him.

FULL SHOT   INT. STABLE

—as Dud gets up quickly, looks about, darts suddenly to a peg in the wall on which the halter hangs, jumps two or three times at it until he dislodges it, runs back to the mare and kneels and slips the halter on her, fumbling with his haste, rises with the end of the rope and crosses quickly to Halliday, rouses him and jams the end of the rope into his hand.

DUD   Stand up! When I holler, jerk up her head!

While Halliday, rising, puzzled, stands, Dud jerks off his miniature ranchman's wide hat, rushes back behind the prone mare, the hat raised to strike the mare across the rump.

DUD   *(to Halliday)* Now! Jerk her head up! Jerk it! *(to the mare, imitating Larry, the hat poised to strike)* Hoy! Hoy—

As he strikes, Mike enters, catches Dud before he can strike.

DUD   *(struggling)* Lemme go! Lemme go! That's the way Doc Hanrahan cured her! Lemme go!

Mike holds him while he struggles. Halliday, holding the rope, looks on amazed. Dud struggles furiously; he is crying now as he tries to beat on the groom who holds him helpless.

DUD   *(crying)* She's going to die! Sultana! Sultana!

DISSOLVE TO:

INT. LARRY'S TACK-ROOM   30 MINUTES LATER

It is almost exactly the same scene as when Dud Teller first appeared at the ranch on his first ride for the doctor. Pelon lies again, his head covered with the blanket and his feet exposed, is in the act of throwing the blanket back and sitting up.

ANOTHER ANGLE   TO INCLUDE FLEECE

—who has just entered, wearing driving coat and gloves.

PELON   *(gently)* He went off with Señora Otis. You knew that, of course?

FLEECE   Yes. I saw his station wagon in the drive. All I want is a competent doctor for my mare.

PELON   *(thoughtfully)* You can't lie at all, can you? You don't even know how.

FLEECE   *(meets his eyes)* All right. I can't. *(rapidly)* But it's not all a lie. I must find him. I think it's anthrax.

PELON   So. *(he starts to throw the blanket back to get up, stops)* If you will go out while I put on my pants.— I am going with you.

FLEECE   You can't. You must stay here. If you'll just tell me where—

PELON   I will go with you. Go out and let me put my pants on, Señorita.

Fleece exits. Pelon swings the blanket back, rises in his long underwear, reaches rapidly for his jeans.

DISSOLVE TO:

EXT. MOUNTAIN ROAD   DAISY'S CAR

—climbing up the road. Daisy is asleep, her head on Larry's shoulder as he drives.

DISSOLVE TO:

EXT. LINDSTROM RANCH   A LITTLE LATER

Larry drives up, stops. Lindstrom has been waiting for him, is already moving toward the car before it stops. In background a half dozen men are waiting also. They are strangers to Larry, in worn clothes; they have the look of small farmers or ranchmen, men who have little but their flocks or herds. Lindstrom's face is worried and strained.

LARRY   *(getting out)* Hello, Gus.

LINDSTROM   I'm glad to see you. If you can't do anything, I'm sunk. I think it's—

LARRY   *(interrupts)* Yeah, I know.

He pauses, looks past Lindstrom.

LARRY AND LINDSTROM   (ANGLE TOWARD MEN)

The shabby men, who have been watching him steadily, hungrily almost, ever since he arrived, have now risen.

LARRY   *(to Lindstrom)* Who're they?

LINDSTROM   Yeah, you never saw them before. They never had any pedigreed horses in Mrs. Astor's pastures yesterday. Between them they probably own two hundred sheep, scattered around between here and the Pass.

LARRY   *(suddenly grave)* You mean—?

LINDSTROM   Yeah. I ain't the first; my two that keeled over last night are just the last. Them fellows have been squatting there ever since midnight, ever since I got you on the phone. They know if you can't help this range, nobody can. If I lose my flock, I can probably build up another one. But if they do— But then, they can always migrate down the valley and pick beans.

LARRY   *(pulls himself together, with hearty encouragement)* Well, maybe we're wrong and they won't need that kind of help. Let's go look at your corpses.

LINDSTROM   *(turns)* Okay. We'll stop at the kitchen first. The Missus has coffee ready.

LARRY   I can use some of it.

ANOTHER ANGLE

—as Larry turns back to the car, starts to take his bag out, pauses. He has forgotten about Daisy, who has not stirred. He looks at her a moment, then shakes her shoulder slightly.

LARRY   Daisy.

DAISY   *(stirs, mutters, still asleep)* Darling. *(turns, reaches her arm for him)* I'm cold.

Larry glances quickly at Lindstrom, who is looking carefully away at the sky. He shakes Daisy harder. She wakes.

LARRY   Snap out of it. Mrs. Lindstrom has coffee ready.

DAISY   *(looks about)* Coffee? At this hour of the night? We'll never go to sleep.

LARRY   *(opens door, pulling her out)* This is tomorrow. Come on.

POOR RANCHERS

—still watching Larry anxiously, as he, Daisy and Lindstrom pass.

LARRY   Morning.

OLD RANCHER   *(speaking for all)* Morning, Doc.

LINDSTROM   You boys come in and have some coffee.

OLD RANCHER   We'll wait.

LARRY   Better come on in. If it's what you think it is, we'll have to do a little talking first. We can do that over the coffee.

INT. LINDSTROM KITCHEN   GROUP

—drinking coffee. Mrs. Lindstrom and two daughters hustling about serving the men and Daisy. Larry, Lindstrom and the spokesman rancher at center. Lamp burning on the table.

OLD RANCHER   It's anthrax all right. I been raising sheep, working among them, for almost seventy years. If you can't help us, nobody can.

LARRY   *(after a moment)* How do you know I've been trying to find an anthrax serum?

The ranchers glance aside at one another, hesitating to speak.

LINDSTROM   I'll tell him then.—One of those horses you're experimenting with—you may remember it—your man, Pelon Reales, brought it in—

LARRY   I remember. Pelon said a man passing through with a remuda gave it to him. I thought at the time it was a pretty sound horse for a man to give away—

LINDSTROM   These men here sent it to you. They and a few others up here. Even up here we heard about what you were trying to do, how you needed horses to make your medicine with. So they took up a collection and bought the horse and sent it by Pelon for you to use.

LARRY   *(looking at the ranchers)* And now you're trying to collect for the horse?

They don't answer.

LINDSTROM   *(after a moment, quietly)* I think you ought to apologize to them for that.

LARRY   So do I. I'm sorry, Pop, and you other boys, too. If I'd known who sent the horse, I'd have thanked you sooner.

LINDSTROM   They didn't send you the horse to be thanked for it, anymore than they sent it for you to make medicine just to save their sheep. It was for all this Range, all this country, for all the livestock everywhere, that, when anthrax strikes them, all they can do is die.

OLD RANCHER   If you need more horses to make more medicine with, we will take up more collections.

LARRY   Thanks. But my serum isn't perfected yet. I can't tell myself what it's going to do. One time it works, then the next time it's worse than anthrax would be; it kills an animal that maybe wouldn't have taken anthrax.

LINDSTROM   *(sets his cup down)* Okay.

LARRY   What do you mean, okay?

LINDSTROM   Have we asked more than that? That's fifty per cent saved. This way, we stand to lose all of them. Okay.

LARRY   But that will be my doing, and I can't make your losses good. I wish I could promise that, but—

LINDSTROM   Look at our faces.

Larry looks about at the sober faces watching him.

LINDSTROM   *(continues)* Is there a man here asking or expecting you to do or guarantee anything, offering to blame you for anything; but just to do what you can?

Larry looks about at the faces, sets his cup down.

LARRY   Okay. Let's go look at those two sheep.

They move, putting their cups on the table as they start toward the door. Mrs. Lindstrom leans and blows out the lamp as the first man opens the door. It is now sunrise.

DISSOLVE TO:

INSIDE SHEEP PEN   SUNRISE

Larry and Lindstrom are kneeling, backs to camera. Larry is doing something with his hands which we cannot see. Lindstrom is watching Larry, intent and sober. Lindstrom's son, Gus, Jr., and a Mexican herder in background. Larry rises; Lindstrom rises too. All three men now watching Larry anxiously as he wipes his hands on a rag. The other ranchers can now be seen in background, all watching Larry with the same gravity.

LARRY That's what it is, Gus.

LINDSTROM *(quietly)* Okay. *(to Gus, Jr.)* All right. Bring up the drove.

Gus, Jr., and the Mexican herder exit, sheep dog following.

LARRY *(to old rancher)* What about it, Pop? You still want to risk it? You haven't lost any sheep yet; it may miss you folks altogether.

OLD RANCHER Okay.

LARRY If I treat them, you'll risk losing half your flocks anyway.

OLD RANCHER Okay.

LARRY *(looks about at others)* That go for all of you?

A MAN Okay, Doc.

LARRY *(starts to take off his coat)* Let me see your hands.

The ranchers hold out their hands for Larry to examine.

LARRY Any of you that don't have any cuts or scratches can help me. The sooner we get through with Gus, the sooner we can get to the next place. Any of you that have cuts or scratches, keep away from here. A man can have anthrax too.

A MAN There's a scratch on your hand, ain't it?

LARRY Yeah. But this stuff knows me.

EXT. RANCH SHEEP MORNING

—as the Mexican herder, Gus, Jr., and the dog move them.

DISSOLVE TO:

SHEEP PEN NOON

Larry, Lindstrom and three ranchers inject a sheep, free it. In background, Daisy and other ranchers watching.

LINDSTROM   *(rises)* That's the last one.

Larry rises slowly. He looks tired, strained. He looks about at the ranchers.

LARRY   All right. Who's next? Who lives the nearest?

OLD RANCHER   *(indicates a man)* Phillips here.

LINDSTROM   *(to Larry)* It's noon. You been up all night. You have some dinner and then get a little sleep first.

LARRY   Mrs. Otis asked Mrs. Lindstrom to fix me a lunch. I'll eat it in the car. I'll have a nap on the way too. Phillips will drive me. *(to the other ranchers)* You other men go on home and get your herds up and have them ready.

The ranchers disperse. Lindstrom's daughter enters with a basin of steaming water, sets it on bench.

LARRY   *(to the girl)* Thanks.

He pours a disinfectant into it, washes his hands carefully, then pours a drop of disinfectant on a scratch on his hand. Daisy approaches, carrying his coat. Larry dries his hands, rolls his sleeve down, takes his coat.

LARRY   Thanks.

He puts on the coat. Lindstrom girl takes the basin out. Larry looks about, sees he and Daisy are alone.

THE TWO   LARRY AND DAISY

LARRY   Gus Junior will drive your car back to town. Thanks for bringing me up.

DAISY   Why is Gus going to town? And why does he have to use my car?

LARRY   Listen. I'm tired. I don't feel like arguing. You're going home.

DAISY   That's good. Being tired'll excuse you for not being able to boss me.

LARRY   What do you suppose your husband'll be thinking, anyway?

DAISY I don't have to suppose. I know. Maybe that's why I'm not going home now:—I don't want to have to listen to him.

LARRY *(after a moment; staring at her while she stares back)* Well, this isn't getting any sheep inoculated. Come on then.

DAISY *(turning)* That's what I think myself.

EXT. LINDSTROM RANCH HOUSE

Daisy's car in foreground. A station wagon is now standing beside it. The station wagon is an expensive outfit, driven by a liveried chauffeur. Lindstrom and Mr. Sneed, a middle-aged man in expensive Abercrombie and Fitch ranching clothes, stand near it, as Larry and Daisy enter.

LINDSTROM *(to Larry)* Mr. Sneed is looking for you.

SNEED *(to Larry)* You Hanrahan? Take your bag and get in my car there. Lindstrom'll send your car down to my place.

LARRY What for?

SNEED I want you to inoculate my stable. I hear some of these scrub sheep up here have got anthrax.

LARRY I see. A professional call. You'll have to take your turn. There are five or six of these scrub sheep owners ahead of you.

He pushes Daisy on to her car, helps her in. Sneed stares at him, taken aback.

SNEED I've got fourteen valuable horses. I'm offering you a hundred dollars apiece to go back with me and inoculate them.

LARRY *(getting into car)* A good horse is easily worth that. As soon as I've finished up here, I'll be glad to earn it. *(to Lindstrom)* Well, Gus. All you can do now is hope.

LINDSTROM Ain't none of us worrying.

Daisy's car drives off. Sneed stares after the car, seething, walks to his station wagon.

LINDSTROM Wait and have some dinner, Mr. Sneed.

Sneed doesn't answer, gets into his station wagon, slams the door behind him. The station wagon drives on.

DISSOLVE TO:

EXT. MOUNTAIN ROAD   SNEED'S STATION WAGON

—rushes along it, swerves slightly, rushes on. When it has passed, we see:

FLEECE'S COUPE

—Pelon driving, Fleece with him—pulled completely out of the narrow road to keep from being run down. It moves on.

DISSOLVE TO:

EXT. LINDSTROM RANCH

Fleece's car has arrived and stopped. Lindstrom stands beside it. Fleece is anxious, strained, tired, still grimly pursuing.

LINDSTROM They went to Phillips' first. But he ain't got but twenty head, so Larry will be done there by now. He's going on to Pop Alvarez' next, so you better go straight there. Take the left hand when you come to the fork. It's about twenty-five miles. But you better stop and eat something first.

FLEECE Thanks, Gus. We must get on.

The car drives on.

DISSOLVE TO:

ALVAREZ RANCH   LATE AFTERNOON

It is still higher in the mountains, not quite as prosperous as Lindstrom's. Daisy is lying in a homemade deck chair thing on the front porch to one side of the door, wrapped in a Navajo blanket, resting. At sound of car offscene she pauses, looks out, reacts, half risen on one elbow.

MED. LONG SHOT   FLEECE AND PELON

Fleece's coupe in background, as they approach the house. They have not seen Daisy yet.

EXT. ALVAREZ RANCH HOUSE   VERANDA

—as Fleece and Pelon cross it toward the door, Daisy watching in background.

DAISY   *(lazily)* Good afternoon.

Fleece and Pelon stop, look toward the voice, recognize her.

DAISY   *(continuing)* You want to see Larry, I suppose. Is Pelon sure he wants to see him—being this far from where his employer supposes him to be?

PELON   I will take that chance, Señora.

Daisy rises lazily, approaches.

DAISY   How far behind is the other car?

FLEECE   What other car?

DAISY   Rick Mallard's of course. He doesn't let his girl run around with Mexican grooms, even if he is a gambler, does he?

While she speaks, Daisy moves in so that she is between Fleece and the door.

AT DOOR   THE THREE   FAVORING DAISY

—as she blocks the door, lazy and smiling.

FLEECE   I must see him.

DAISY   I'm sure you can—when he wakes up. We've been inoculating thousands of sheep all day but I'm sure we can squeeze you in somewhere.

FLEECE   *(starts forward)* Will you please get out of the way?

DAISY   *(gives way)* If you insist.

INT. ALVAREZ RANCH HOUSE   LIVING ROOM

Daisy crosses the room toward a door, Fleece and Pelon following. Daisy is putting on a show; her air is possessive, wifely.

DAISY   Don't blame me now. He's such a bear when he's wakened suddenly—

She reaches the door, opens it, enters. Others follow.

INT. ROUGH RANCH BEDROOM

Larry asleep on a cot. He looks tired, needs a shave, is sleeping with heavy exhaustion. Daisy crosses to him.

DAISY *(shakes him)* Darling.

Larry mutters, turns away. She shakes him again.

DAISY Do wake up. And don't swear at me. It's Miss Teller, on a matter of life and death—

Larry wakes, takes a second to get himself together, sees Fleece, is about to speak to her when he sees Pelon behind her.

LARRY *(grimly; to Pelon)* What are you doing up here? Who told you to leave the ranch?

PELON *(their eyes clash)* I am trying to forget.

FLEECE *(hurriedly)* He brought me up. It's Sultana again. She's—

LARRY *(acidly)* Yeah, your mare. All I needed was my hat to get her up. Couldn't Pelon do that without coming eighty miles from where I want him to be?

FLEECE Will you please not tell me again that all she's got is colic? I don't think I could bear it this time.

DAISY *(to Fleece)* You aren't next, darling. There are three ahead of you. *(to Larry)* No, four, counting that Sneed man who offered you a thousand dollars.

FLEECE *(disregarding Daisy)* I wouldn't be here if there was anything else I could do. You don't hate my being here anymore than I do—

DAISY *(to Fleece)* We don't hate your being here, darling. On the contrary—

LARRY Will you both hush a minute?

They hush, watching him. He continues to Fleece.

LARRY All right. I've got three more herds up here to treat. I'll stop and see what Sneed's screaming about on the way down. As soon as I'm done there, I'll come straight to your place. *(to Pelon)* And you get to blazes back home too—

FLEECE *(interrupts)* That'll be tomorrow night—maybe. Provided your friends will let you—

DAISY *(to Fleece)* Really, darling, after the showing your horses made yesterday, surely an extra day and night won't matter—

Fleece, turning quickly, slaps Daisy, who falls back.

DAISY Why, you—

She hurls herself at Fleece. They grapple for a moment as Daisy claws at Fleece's face. Without moving, Larry lies easily on the cot, watching them.

LARRY That's right. Get it out of your systems and let me finish my nap.

Suddenly Daisy goes flying across the room and into the wall, stops, staring at Fleece, who now has the marks of her fingers across her cheek. Pelon watches, inscrutable.

DAISY Why, you kicked me!

She rushes at Fleece again, they grapple, Fleece holding Daisy off as Daisy claws at her. Daisy sinks her teeth into Fleece's wrist. With an effort Fleece flings her off. Pelon catches Daisy, holds her struggling.

LARRY *(to Pelon)* Take her out and keep her out.

PELON *(as he drags Daisy, struggling, toward the door)* I think I have forgotten now.

They exit. Daisy's screams cease. Larry still lies on the cot, looking at Fleece, who stands panting a little.

LARRY Women! Go on back home. As soon as I finish up here—

FLEECE *(rouses, turns toward the door)* Don't bother.

LARRY Okay. If you'd taken time to decide that before you left home, you'd have saved yourself the trip. Let alone taking Pelon away from that stable full of dynamite we've got.

FLEECE *(stops, turns back; after a moment, trying to be calmer)* At least you could advise me. What shall I do?

LARRY Put something on that wrist then. She might have hydrophobia.

Fleece stares at him, furious now, gets hold of herself with an effort.

FLEECE The first thing you do in that case is destroy the dog that bit you, isn't it? *(turns toward door again)* Maybe I'll take that advice—

Larry starts to get up as she hurries across the room.

LARRY Fleece!

She runs toward the door. He leaps up from the cot, beats her to the door, catches her in his arms.

FLEECE Get out of the way!

LARRY All right. If you'll quit acting like a child.

FLEECE I'm not going to hurt your girl friend. I'm going home; I have a sick mare there.

LARRY *(releases her)* Okay. I'll get to your place as soon as I'm through up here.

But Fleece has not waited. She hurries out. Larry looks after her, turns and starts back toward the cot. Sound of motor outside. He stops and listens as the motor starts violently, then sound of Fleece's coupe as it rushes violently away. Larry goes to the cot, looks longingly at it, but instead of lying down he lifts his bag from beside it, takes his hat and coat from the wall, is putting the coat on as he crosses toward the door.

EXT. ALVAREZ RANCH HOUSE   ON FRONT PORCH

Fleece's coupe is almost out of sight down the road. Daisy stands looking after it as Larry enters.

DAISY Toots is driving now.

LARRY I heard her. Get your coat.

DAISY Aren't you going to finish your nap?

LARRY What nap?

EXT. TELLER STABLES   NIGHT

Fleece's coupe enters, fast, skids to a stop as Fleece brakes it and jumps out, hurries toward stable door.

AT STABLE DOOR   MIKE AND DUD

—standing, looking at Fleece as she runs in. Mike's face is grave, Dud's is tense, wild-looking, streaked with dirt and dried tears. Fleece seems to read the bad news, stops.

DUD   *(wildly)* He never come!

FLEECE   *(moves again, quickly, though her voice is calm; to Mike)* When was it?

MIKE   *(soberly)* Yesterday. About dark. I notified the health officers—

DUD   *(crying again)* They burned her! They burned Sultana. Because Hanrahan never come—

He runs suddenly, his face frantic. Mike grabs at him, vainly. Fleece catches him as he tries to dart past her.

DUD   *(struggling)* Lemme go! Durn Hanrahan! Durn him! I'll fix him for killing Sultana—

FLEECE   *(holding him)* Dud. Dud. *(he stops struggling; to Mike)* Has he been to bed at all?

MIKE   I couldn't do anything with him.

FLEECE   *(gentle yet firm; to Dud)* Come on to bed now. *(begins to lead him out)*

DUD   *(resists)* No! We got to fix Hanrahan—

FLEECE   *(draws him on)* Come on now. I'll sit by you.

They go out.

DISSOLVE TO:

INT. DUD'S BEDROOM

Dud is in bed, Fleece sitting beside the bed. He has been crying again, but is asleep now. Fleece, seeing he is asleep, turns light off, leans back in the chair, closes her eyes, opens them, turns her head. The door opens quietly, Mike stands in it.

MIKE   You better go to bed yourself.

FLEECE   I will.

Mike exits. Fleece closes her eyes again.

LAP DISSOLVE TO:

SAME SCENE   NEXT MORNING

Fleece is now asleep in the chair. Dud wakes, yawns, remembers yesterday, starts up, sees Fleece, becomes quiet and cautious, gets up cautiously, tiptoes to chair, gathers up his shirt and levis and hat, tiptoes out.

DISSOLVE TO:

EXT. STALLION ROAD RANCH   AT GATE   DAY

Larry is walking up the drive, carying his bag. Daisy's car is driving away in background. He is still unshaven, tired looking.

EXT. STALLION ROAD RANCH HOUSE   LARRY

—is walking quickly toward his parked station wagon in its usual place before the house when Pelon appears suddenly and quietly from beyond the station wagon, where he has obviously been waiting and watching for Larry's return. Larry sees him, pauses, then opens the door of the station wagon and starts to get in.

LARRY   (*over shoulder to Pelon*) I'm going to run up to Teller's. I'll be back in a couple of hours.

PELON   (*calmly*) We can save ourselves that trouble now.

Larry stops, a take almost, then he looks at Pelon, who at that moment turns his head and looks out as sound of hooves comes OVER.

PELON   (*calmly*) You're going to get it from headquarters now.

Larry turns. Dud gallops in, on the same pony, still bareback, the pony spent again. Dud's face is still dirty and streaked, frantic and wild-looking. He flings himself down, rushes at Larry, begins to hammer on Larry with his fists as high as he can reach.

LARRY AND DUD   BY STATION WAGON

Dud hammering at Larry, who holds him off. Sound of car offscene.

DUD   You killed her! I hope that ten thousand dollars chokes you—!

Fleece's coupe enters background and stops. Fleece gets out.

ANOTHER ANGLE

Pelon now holding Dud as he stops struggling, crying hard now. Fleece watching, Larry recovering.

 FLEECE　*(quietly, to Pelon)* Thank you, Pelon.

She comes up, takes Dud's arm, leads him toward the coupe.

 PELON　That is right, Señorita. Take him with you. We will send the pony home.

 FLEECE　*(over shoulder, leading Dud on to coupe, from which the stableboy is now getting out)* Thank you. I brought Pedro with me.

 PELON　I will give him a saddle—

 FLEECE　*(as Dud gets into coupe)* Thanks. We won't trouble you.

She gets into coupe, starts it, drives on. Pedro approaches the pony.

 LARRY　*(to Pedro)* Better take a saddle.

 PEDRO　I'll be all right.

He gets up, and rides on, exits. Larry turns, goes back to the station wagon, feels Pelon watching him, pauses and looks back.

 LARRY　*(harshly)* I suppose you've got a comment to make on this too.

 PELON　*(calmly)* I can try again to forget.

Their eyes clash for an instant, then Larry gets into the station wagon, starts the engine.

 LARRY　*(to Pelon)* I'm going to run into town a minute. Be back after a while.

He drives away, Pelon looking after him, inscrutable.

DISSOLVE TO:

INT. COURTHOUSE　　CLOSE ON DOOR　　DAY

Lettered on the frosted glass:

COUNTY RECORDER

INT. RECORDER'S OFFICE   LARRY AND CLERK

Larry standing, facing clerk across a desk, a paper between them which the clerk is examining with interest.

CLERK   *(in tone of surprise)* Lady Rea II. I didn't know you'd sell her.

LARRY   *(shortly)* Selling horses is my business.

CLERK   She's got a good chance to win that All-Western ten thousand, hasn't she?

LARRY   *(short and dry)* I think so.

CLERK   Miss Teller's making a good buy then.

LARRY   *(same tone)* I hope so. I like my customers to be satisfied with what I sell them.

The clerk draws ledger toward him, begins to record the deed of sale.

DISSOLVE TO:

EXT. VILLAGE STREET   LARRY   IN HIS STATION WAGON

—about to start it. As he is about to put it into gear, he looks out of scene, reacts. Fleece's coupe passes him. She is alone in it, does not see him, or at least gives no indication. She is driving fast. She goes on. He starts his car, drives away.

DISSOLVE TO:

EXT. MALLARD'S TAVERN   DAY

Fleece drives up, stops her car, gets out, approaches door, enters.

INT. MALLARD'S TAVERN   BAR

Fleece enters, passes through it, seems to know exactly where she is going. Barman speaks to her, she does not seem to hear him.

INT. MALLARD'S PRIVATE OFFICE

Mallard, seated at desk, rises as the door opens and Fleece enters without knocking, leans against it.

CLOSE SHOT   FLEECE

—looking at Mallard with that bright, tense, too calm expression.

FLEECE   Hello, Rick.

MALLARD AND FLEECE

MALLARD   When did you get back?

FLEECE   *(hysteria showing a little; still calm though outwardly)*
Yes. I don't know.

MALLARD   *(beginning to notice her state)* How's Sultana?

FLEECE   *(lightly, impersonal)* Oh, you mean my mare. She's dead.
Your friend Larry Hanrahan killed her—

CLOSER SHOT   THE TWO

Mallard moves quickly in, takes her by both arms as if to hold her up:
is anxious, alarmed.

FLEECE   *(continuing)* He probably killed that mare of Harrison
Sneed's too. So now he won't have any competition at Sierra. That's
it, you see: he did it not because he doesn't like me, but just to win
a ten thousand dollar prize—

She begins to shake and tremble, fighting it.

MALLARD   Fleece! Stop it! Stop it!

FLEECE   That's right, Rick. Hold me. Hold me.

He holds her. But that is not what she wants either. She puts her arms
around him, pulls him close and hard. She is kissing him before he
knows what she wants of him.

FLEECE   Yes, Rick. Yes.

MALLARD   You mean . . . you'll marry me?

FLEECE   *(holding him)* Yes, Rick.

MALLARD   *(draws his head back, watching her)* Don't kid me,
Fleece. I'm too old for that now. Maybe I couldn't stand it—

FLEECE *(draws him down to kiss)* Does this feel like I'm kidding you—lying to you—?

He kisses her. They hold it, as we—

FADE OUT.

FADE IN

EXT. LARRY'S STABLE   DAY

Pelon and two stablemen are loading Larry's prize mare, Lady Rea II, into a truck. Pelon fusses over the loading like an old hen. Larry stands beside the truck.

PELON *(in Spanish; to helpers)* Easy, fools! Easy! *(in English)* What do you think this is: a ten dollar blind mule you're shipping to the glue factory?

LARRY Shove her along, though. I want her to be over the Pass before night. *(he goes to the front of the truck bed, steps up, faces the mare, speaks soothingly)* Come on here. What's the matter with you—a woman that don't want to go to town. Maybe Pelon'll buy you a new hat, when he gets there.

THE MARE   (FROM LARRY'S ANGLE)

—watches him a moment, her ears cocked, nervous. Then she surges, steps into the truck, comes up to Larry's hand and nuzzles him.

ANOTHER ANGLE   (TO INCLUDE THE OTHERS)

Larry watching. Pelon supervises while the helpers close the end gate, halter the mare forward in the truck. Pelon looks off at the sky, steps down from the truck.

PELON *(to Larry)* You said well. See that?

They all look off at:

THE SKY

—toward the distant mountains. Clouds gathered about the Pass.

THE GROUP   BY TRUCK

PELON   That's snow.

LARRY   Maybe not. But she'll be through the Pass before night. That is, if you'll ever get her started.

PELON   Some of the mares left yesterday.

LARRY   (*needling Pelon, who does not know he gave mare to Fleece*) Yeah, Miss Teller's did. Not for Sierra though. That what you mean?

Pelon's attitude has changed completely, as his speech from here on shows. There is something curious in his manner. The fact is, he has learned by backdoor rumor that Fleece is going to marry Rick, so he has given her up as a possible wife for Larry. But he still does not approve of Daisy, though this is not so important now that he assumes Larry has lost Fleece.

PELON   If we're expected to cure the whole Range, let them put off the anthrax until we have perfected our serum.

LARRY   We haven't got anything to cure snowblindness either. You better get her started. We'll drive through tonight.

PELON   Then maybe we can spend the day hunting a cure for snowblindness. (*turns; to helpers*) Vayos, amigos.

The two helpers get into the cab of the truck. It drives out. Larry and Pelon watch it out. Then Larry turns, moves on, Pelon following.

PELON AND LARRY

—moving.

PELON   We did save some of Lindstrom's sheep.

Larry stops, turns, looks curiously back at Pelon.

PELON   So our serum does work sometimes.

LARRY   (*after a moment*) What's the matter now? You having to start trying to forget all over?

PELON   (*largely*) Maybe somebody else will have to do a little forgetting too. After all, we can produce just so much serum, and no more. We couldn't get around to everyone.

TWO SHOT (FAVORING PELON)

PELON And of course we can't be expected to make our losses good—especially when we didn't even get around to treating the horse, no matter how serious the loss might have been to the owner—

LARRY So what? Is this an apology?

PELON *(shrugs)* After all, a man can only do what he must do.

LARRY *(evenly)* Since you've already interfered in this without any request from anybody I know of, we might clear it up a little further.

ANOTHER ANGLE THE TWO (FAVORING LARRY)

LARRY You seem to have overlooked something. I'm not in love with Miss Teller. You'll probably find a lot of guys around here who are not in love with Miss Teller—since attending to other people's affairs seems to be your principal business these days.

While Pelon watches him, he turns and starts out, speaks back over his shoulder.

LARRY *(continuing)* Be ready to start about three o'clock. I'll pick up Mrs. Otis and be back before then. *(he stops as though at a sudden thought, turns back as Pelon watches him)* Or maybe you'll change your mind now and not go at all?

PELON Why not? You've never minded a witness yet, have you?

LARRY I see. What I've got is a chaperone.

PELON *(after a moment)* That's right. Come back and hit me again. It seems to make you feel good.

MED. CLOSE SHOT LARRY AND PELON

LARRY *(after a moment)* All right. What is it? You don't have to like her. But why do you have to work at it?

PELON I don't mind you being what they call in Hollywood a wolf. But I hate to see you be a blind one.

LARRY You've gone a little far to stop on just that. Let's have the rest of it.

PELON She's dangerous. She's poison. She's worse than that: she's dynamite.

LARRY *(after a moment; turns)* Be ready about three. You may be right about that snow.

He exits.

DISSOLVE TO:

INT. LARRY'S LABORATORY TACK-ROOM   AFTERNOON

Larry, dressed for trip in tweed suit, necktie, etc., is busy at his table. His open black professional bag sits on the table; he is busy transferring anthrax cultures from their tubes into a vacuum bottle. He now wears rubber gloves, which we have not seen him wear before. These, and his whole manner, denote a care in handling the poisonous serum which we have not seen before. Daisy and Pelon, dressed also for the trip, are watching. That is, Daisy is watching, Pelon is helping to pack various things they will take with them. He is quite dressed up, in his Sunday clothes. There is something, not quite comical, not quite pathetic, in his finery.

DAISY I thought you used all your serum on those sheep.

PELON He spent last night making this batch.

DAISY Not all of it though. You don't follow him everywhere.

PELON *(busy)* The señora is much too beautiful to need to lie away her good name. But in this case, I myself saw the light burning down here, even after I went to bed.

DAISY So one dingy electric light protects my reputation in spite of me.

PELON One tiny little unforeseen electric light often does that for beautiful ladies.

DAISY But not forever—as you'll find out, if you just spy long enough. *(to Larry)* Are you taking this stuff with us?

LARRY   Yeah. To Professor Hoffmeyer, at the University. He wants to look at it.

DAISY   Then you and your faithful watchdog can do the packing. I'll ride in a car with it if I have to, but I'm not going to stay here with it flying around loose in the air. *(going out)* Please hurry though.

She goes out. Her bag and gloves still lie on the bench.

MED. SHOT   PELON AND LARRY

Larry corks the vacuum bottle, sets it down, takes up a cloth and moistens it from a phial of disinfectant marked poison. Pelon watches him.

PELON   I want to apologize for this morning.

LARRY   *(carefully wiping the vacuum bottle with the cloth, pauses)* So you're starting all over again to forget, are you?

PELON   *(still with that curious tone)* Oh, you mean Señora Otis. Yes, I have forgotten that.

LARRY   Then what do you mean?

PELON   So you haven't heard yet.

LARRY   What are you hinting at?

PELON   Nothing. It will not be news anywhere by tomorrow.— Here. It's already three o'clock.

He takes hold of the rim of one of Larry's gloves, carefully yet firmly; apparently they have done this often before, as Larry sets the vacuum bottle down and lets Pelon strip off both the gloves and put them away while Larry moistens the cloth again from the bottle and wipes his hands off and then hands the cloth to Pelon, who wipes his own hands and puts the cloth away with the gloves.

FULL SHOT   INT. TACK-ROOM

Larry is now concentrating on a scratch on his wrist. Pelon is packing the vacuum bottle into the medicine bag. Daisy enters, as Larry is pouring carefully from the phial onto the cut.

DAISY Aren't you ready yet? *(she sees what Larry is doing)* Are you messing with that nasty stuff with a cut hand?

PELON He is taking care of that now.

DAISY But how do you know what's in the bottle is strong enough?

LARRY *(corks the phial)* Let's hope it is.

He drops the phial into the bag, then takes up a big hypodermic needle.

DAISY *(watching)* What's that?

LARRY *(puts the needles carefully into the bag)* That's the anthrax itself. After all, Hoffmeyer's got to know what I'm trying to cure. *(he closes the bag)* Ready.

DAISY *(turns)* Let's do get out of here.

She exits. Larry and Pelon gather up bag, coats, etc., to follow.

DISSOLVE TO:

EXT. MOUNTAIN HIGHWAY   LARRY'S STATION WAGON

Larry is driving, Daisy beside him, Pelon behind them in back seat. They are in the mountains now, the highway ascending. A car approaches, coming down. As it passes, Pelon leans suddenly forward.

PELON Look there.

SHOT OF PASSING CAR

We see small patches of snow on the windshield and top.

LARRY'S STATION WAGON   ON MOUNTAIN HIGHWAY

DAISY I love snow. It's so cozy.

PELON Not up here in the Pass.

DAISY Why not? With two brave strong men to protect me, keep me warm?

PELON *(to Larry)* You see it?

LARRY Yeah.

DISSOLVE TO:

INT. LUNCH-STAND AT COUNTER LARRY, DAISY, PELON DUSK

—just finishing sandwiches and coffee. Daisy takes cigarette from Larry, who snaps on lighter, then lays a bill on the counter, which the counterman takes up.

COUNTERMAN Better put your chains on. Highway truck just went up with a load of sand.

Larry lights his own cigarette, puts lighter away, stands up. Daisy follows. Counterman turns, rings cash register.

LARRY It's too early for deep snow yet.

COUNTERMAN (*turns, lays change before Larry who pockets it*) That Pass don't care what day the calendar says it is. Take my advice—

LARRY (*turns*) Thanks.

They follow him out.

EXT. LUNCH-STAND

Several cars are parked before it, including Larry's station wagon. Two of the cars are pointed down the grade. Both have patches of snow on them. Pelon slows, looking at the snow quietly. Larry goes on to the station wagon. Daisy with him.

PELON The counterman is right.

LARRY (*about to get in*) So were you.

PELON What do you think?

LARRY (*waiting for Pelon; inscrutable*) I'd say it was snow.

DAISY (*getting into car*) It's just snow. That's all.

Pelon shrugs, follows, gets in. The station wagon starts.

DAISY And I love snow.

DISSOLVE TO:

THE PASS LARRY'S STATION WAGON (SNOWING) NIGHT

It is snowing, the earth is covered. The station wagon has been halted by waving lights. A policeman, snow-covered, with flashlight, leans in opened window. Beyond the policeman a car lies on its side, wrecked, other lights around it.

LARRY *(to cop)* Anybody hurt?

POLICEMAN *(drily)* Not yet. Better turn around and get back out of here.

DAISY *(lightly)* Oh, come, Commissioner. Just one little wreck— probably the driver's fault anyway—

POLICEMAN *(drily)* This ain't but one snow, either. *(to Larry)* Better get out of here.

LARRY Is that an order?

POLICEMAN Tourist, huh?

LARRY I live in the valley. Been using this Pass all my life.

POLICEMAN Okay, brother. It's at your own risk, though.

LARRY Thanks. *(closes window, puts car into gear)*

PELON *(to Daisy)* I hope you still love snow, Señora.

The car moves on.

DAISY I don't think it will trouble you when I don't.

DISSOLVE TO:

LONELY MOUNTAINS   LARRY'S STATION WAGON   (SNOWING) NIGHT

The station wagon has stopped. Deep snow all about.

LARRY We're off the road.

DAISY Don't be silly. We can't be.

LARRY Didn't you feel that stump back there? This is an old logger's cutoff.

PELON But somebody has gone through ahead of us. See the tracks.

LARRY You mean, somebody's in here ahead of us.

DAISY *(anxiously)* What do you mean?

They pay no attention to her. They don't look worried so much as grimly alert. Larry starts the car again. It lurches into the snow.

PELON At least we don't have to worry. We can't turn around.

LARRY *(fighting wheel as car lurches and plunges on)* There is an abandoned trapper's cabin on ahead—if we get that far.

DAISY Oh, a house. Then we'll be all right.

LARRY *(fighting wheel)* I said abandoned.

DAISY We can always send Pelon back to the highway for help.

PELON It is you who loves snow, Señora—not I.

The car lurches on as Larry fights the wheel.

DAISY *(anxiously)* What do you mean, if we get that far?

Larry doesn't answer, fighting the wheel, staring intently ahead as the car lurches on. Suddenly he stops it.

LARRY'S STATION WAGON   BEHIND A HUGE DRIFT

Larry has just stopped the station wagon. From their angle and beneath the drift can be seen the shape of a stalled car.

LARRY This. *(starts to get out; rapidly to Pelon)* Come on—if they're not already—

Larry and Pelon get out of station wagon, hurry toward the stalled car.

LARRY AND PELON   BY STALLED CAR

Quickly Larry brushes snow off, jerks open the door, more snow tumbles over him as he leans quickly in. The car is empty.

LARRY It's empty.

He is about to close the door, when Pelon, with a curious expression, leans past him and looks inside the car.

LARRY *(continuing)* Let's hope he knew about the old cabin too. This is the end of the line, for tonight, anyway. Get Daisy.

Pelon withdraws slowly from the car, looks at Larry.

PELON   You know whose car it is?

LARRY   *(impatiently)* No. Go get Mrs. Otis.— Get the robe and lunchbox.

PELON   It's Rick Mallard's.

LARRY   So what?

PELON   I imagine Miss Teller's with him. They left for Stateline this afternoon to be married.

LARRY   *(after a moment)* So that's what you've been hinting at all afternoon.

PELON   I? I've been forgetting.

He turns back toward the station wagon. Larry stares after him, then suddenly Larry turns and flounders away in the snow.

NEAR STATION WAGON   PELON

—has paused and turned, watching Larry as he flounders on away from the road, trying to run. Daisy leans from the station wagon, looking after Larry.

DAISY   Where's he going? Whose car is that?

PELON   Rick Mallard's. Miss Teller is with him. You cannot see the rice and the old shoes for the snow.

DAISY   *(quickly)* They're married?

PELON   *(opens the door for her to get out)* We have not reached the state line yet. Larry says to come on.

DAISY   *(quickly, with fear almost)* Call him back. We're going to get out of here.

PELON   How? It's not Larry and me who love snow.

DAISY   *(gets hold of herself)* Yes. Maybe Miss Teller won't, either.

She gets out of station wagon. Pelon pulls out a robe, lunchbox, Daisy's overnight bag, Larry's medicine bag. Daisy is already floundering on toward where Larry has disappeared. Pelon follows her.

REVERSE ANGLE   LARRY

—has stopped, is waiting until Daisy and Pelon struggle up to him. Daisy's face is strained, grim. Her voice though is viciously silken.

DAISY   *(vicious and silken)* Hello. We thought you'd rushed on to save Toots from a fate worse than death.

LARRY   *(noncommittal; takes her arm)* They're already in the cabin, I guess. You're the one risking frostbite. Come on.

DAISY   *(holds back, stares at him, deadly serious now)* Are they married yet?

LARRY   You can ask them in a minute. Come on.

DISSOLVE TO:

INT. CABIN   NIGHT

It is very crude: a fireplace, a rough shelf nailed to wall, a crude bunk nailed to wall, a few crude seats made of "bolts" sawn from a log, etc. A small fire burns on hearth.

Fleece is peering out the snow-banked and frosted window. She wears her coat and hat, holds coat about her, looks worried; she had not quite counted on this. She's peering out the window now with an expression of shock, almost terror. Rick, behind her, is looking out too, shocked but grim rather than alarmed.

A sound outside, feet approaching. Sound beyond the door as it opens. Fleece turns quickly, shrinking, quickly regaining command, Rick turning slower but very watchful, as the door opens and Daisy, followed by Pelon, enters.

DAISY   May we came in? *(she says "came," not "come." She is ribbing them, outwardly cheery and pleasant, but vicious inside)* Thank you.

FLEECE   Of course. Hello, Pelon.

DAISY   Thank you again. *(with mock surprise)* It's Rick Mallard. Isn't this cozy!

PELON   *(to Fleece)* I am sorry of this, Señorita.

But he is not sorry at all. Daisy sees it, blazes at him.

DAISY *(to Pelon)* Then don't try so hard to look like it.

Fleece doesn't answer, still watching the door. Larry enters. He carries a limb, brush. He doesn't look at Fleece, he speaks to no one as he crosses and flings the firewood down beside the hearth.

LARRY *(harshly to Rick)* Is this all the wood you've got in? If you want to freeze, you could do it a lot more comfortably in the car.

DAISY Don't be crude, darling. A bride and groom?

MALLARD *(moving)* I forgot my flashlight. I was just going back to the car for it—

LARRY *(turning)* I've got it.

He turns toward the door, still not looking at Fleece, who is still watching him, catches Daisy's eye on her, recovers as Rick follows Larry toward the door.

DAISY *(loudly)* But we hear you're not married yet. Isn't it exciting?

Fleece turns suddenly toward the door as Rick follows Larry out. Pelon moves to follow.

PELON I think it will be better if we all carry wood for a while.

DAISY *(following)* Why not?

They exit.

EXT. CABIN   LARRY AND RICK   (SNOW)   NIGHT

Larry, followed by Rick, reaches woodpile, starts to pick up logs, brush. Rick watches him.

MALLARD Well—

LARRY *(beginning to stoop)* Well what? *(Rick looks at his back; Larry pauses)* What do you want me to do? Apologize for being here?

MALLARD No. It was the snow.

LARRY Then what? Are you apologizing for the snow?

MALLARD   No.

LARRY   Then what do you want?

MALLARD   Nothing. I didn't throw my chance away.

LARRY   So what are you aching about?

MALLARD   Nothing.

LARRY   Okay, then. *(he stoops to woodpile)*

After a moment Rick stoops also. They begin to load their arms with wood.

EXT. CABIN   FLEECE AND DAISY   (SNOW)   NIGHT

Fleece is tugging at a half-buried branch. Daisy enters behind her, stands watching as Fleece tugs to free the limb.

DAISY   *(after a moment)* That's mine, darling. I picked it out on the way up from the car.

FLEECE   *(turns)* All right. Are you just claiming it, or do you intend to help getting it to the cabin?

DAISY   Oh, I always help. That is, as soon as my prior claim is admitted. *(she comes forward)*

Fleece waits for her to grasp the limb. Daisy does not do so, stands again. After a moment Fleece, seeing she is not going to help, tugs at the limb, frees it from the snow.

DAISY   I'm glad to see your arm's all right.

FLEECE   *(pauses)* What about my arm?

DAISY   *(airily)* Where it got bitten: remember?

She approaches slowly, takes hold of the limb, Fleece still holding her end of the limb, facing Daisy, who stares at her.

DAISY   *(continuing)* Did it ever occur to you that a human being might be poison too? *(softly, staring at Fleece)* That I am poison? Dangerous?

FLEECE   Yes. I know you are.

DAISY   *(softly, staring at Fleece, insistent)* Very dangerous?

FLEECE   At least you won't have to worry tonight. And tomorrow we'll be—

Daisy interrupts, intent, jeering, prodding, reminding Fleece of what tomorrow means, forcing her hand.

DAISY   —safely married?—

FLEECE   Yes.

DAISY   (*pressing her*) Because you don't love Larry, you love Rick Mallard.

FLEECE   Yes. (*louder*) Yes. I love Rick Mallard.

DAISY   Take my advice and keep on loving him. (*releases her end of the limb, turns, brushing her hands*) Bring it on. We'll need it tonight.

She goes on. After a moment Fleece raises the limb onto her shoulder, follows.

EXT. NEARER CABIN   FLEECE AND PELON   (SNOW)   NIGHT

Fleece is standing in the snow, the limb over her shoulder, staring off, as Pelon enters, carrying another limb over his shoulder. She does not move when he stops beside her, staring off in same direction.

PELON   What did she say to you, Señorita?

FLEECE   (*staring after Daisy*) Why did you bring them here? (*recovers, pulls herself together*) Make him leave. Remind him of his serum or something. A man can make it back to the highway on foot yet.

PELON   But Señora Otis is not a man—though I won't say there are not some here who might wish she was—for a little while—

FLEECE   (*grimly, drily*) I can handle Mrs. Otis.

PELON   (*watches her*) Yes. Because it's not Mrs. Otis being here that worries you.

Fleece looks quickly away, covers her thoughts, staring off again.

PELON   Give me this tree. I'll carry it.

Fleece, staring off, lowers the limb until the end rests in the snow. But she still holds it, staring off. Pelon still watches her averted face.

PELON *(continuing)* Because you're not worrying about anything. You love Rick Mallard. You're going to marry him— *(he picks up one end of the limb)* Let's get on to the house; it's cold—

Suddenly, as he picks up his end of the limb, Fleece releases the other end, is already moving; by the time Pelon regains his balance, she has already gone, leaving him with the limb. He manages with some difficulty to shoulder the second limb, follows with both.

EXT. NEAR CABIN DOOR   MALLARD, LARRY, FLEECE   (SNOW)
NIGHT

Mallard enters, loaded with wood, followed by Larry with a load. They are about to pass when Fleece appears suddenly beside a tree.

FLEECE Doctor Hanrahan—

Larry and Rick see her, pause.

LARRY *(to Mallard)* It's okay if I speak to your bride a minute?

FLEECE Please, Rick.

MALLARD *(after a moment, starts on)* Of course.

FLEECE Thanks, Rick.

Mallard exits. Larry waits, facing Fleece, still carrying his load of wood.

THE TWO   LARRY AND FLEECE

LARRY Now what?

FLEECE Get out of here, will you?

LARRY Don't make me laugh. Daisy and Pelon and I were lucky to get here. So were you and Mallard, for that matter.

FLEECE *(changes over)* I know. I'm sorry. What are we going to do?

LARRY *(cold, unchanged)* What do you think? Stay here. Try to keep from freezing—which won't be hard; we will stay warm trying to keep that fire burning all night.

INT. CABIN   DAISY AND MALLARD   NIGHT

Daisy is standing before the fire, skirt raised slightly, one foot extended to blaze as Mallard enters. She doesn't look up until he comes to fire, dumps his load of wood. Then she looks up, looks back, sees he is alone.

DAISY   Where's your pal?

MALLARD   Outside.

DAISY   *(suddenly, after a second)* Oh. He's bringing the bride, is he?

MALLARD   Why not?

DAISY   *(stares at him a second)* My hero.

She crosses toward door, exits, closes the door slowly behind her.

EXT. CABIN   LARRY AND FLEECE   (SNOW)   NIGHT

—still facing each other as before.

LARRY   The snowplow'll get through in the morning and clear the road and you and Mallard can go on to wherever you're going and get married. What are you worrying about?

FLEECE   *(changed again, defiant)* All right. I'm not worrying.

LARRY   Then shut up, will you?

FLEECE   *(angry now)* Because I love Rick Mallard! At least he's not a murderer . . .

LARRY   *(lowers the wood slowly)* A murderer, am I?

FLEECE   Yes! You killed my mare—

Larry lets the wood fall and scatter on the snow, unheeded now, as he steps toward her.

LARRY   And you love Rick Mallard, huh?

FLEECE   *(holds her ground, defies him)* Yes!

LARRY   *(grabs her in his arms)* Is that so?

FLEECE   *(struggling)* Yes!

She frees one hand, suddenly and savagely slashes at him, but he catches it, holds her helpless and panting, still struggling.

LARRY Huh? Is it?

FLEECE Yes! Y——

He kisses her, smothers the word, holds her face to his while she struggles. Suddenly she is kissing him back, but this too is violent, like the struggling.

DAISY'S VOICE *(offscene; cool, derisive)* Break, children. There goes the bell.

WIDER ANGLE (TO INCLUDE DAISY)

—in background before cabin, watching them.

DAISY The cash customers are getting impatient . . .

Fleece walks past her, enters the cabin. After a moment Larry picks up his wood, follows.

DAISY *(as he passes her)* Did you like it?

He enters the cabin, making no answer. She follows. The door closes.

INT. CABIN

—as Larry, followed by Daisy, enters. The others are huddled about the fire, still wearing their coats, etc.

LARRY *(to all, harshly)* Come on, now. Get those coats off. What are you going to do when we run out of wood along toward morning and it really gets cold?

MED. CLOSE LARRY

—kneeling, facing the wall. Above him hang his, Pelon's and Daisy's coats from nails on pegs. Below them sit Daisy's and Fleece's suit-cases, and Larry's black medical bag. The bag is open. Larry has removed the small phial of disinfectant which he was using in his laboratory in the tack-room and is again rapidly treating the scratch on his wrist with the liquid. His body conceals what he is doing, in a second now he will be done. But Mallard enters, carrying his and Fleece's coats, is about to hang them on two other nails or pegs when he sees what Larry is doing, pauses only a moment as Larry puts the

phial back into the bag and closes it. Sound OVER as the two women
and Pelon spread the food before the fire.

MALLARD (*moves again and hangs up the two coats; quietly to
Larry*) I hope you won't need any outside help with that either.

LARRY (*rising; quietly, noncommittal*) I guess I won't.

He turns. Mallard follows.

DISSOLVE TO:

GROUP SHOT   INT. CABIN

A robe and a cloth have been spread. Larry's lunchbox has been
opened. Food, sandwiches, fruit, etc., are placed about the cloth. The
five people sit on the floor around it. They have finished eating. Pelon
is opening a wine bottle. The others have drinking receptacles ready:
a few patent cups. Larry is using the shell of a flashlight from which
battery, bulb, reflector, have been removed. Pelon has a clean gradu-
ated chemist's flagon from Larry's medicine kit.

MALLARD (*to Pelon; indicates flagon*) Are you sure that thing's
sterilized?

PELON (*opening bottle*) No, Señor. But I hope to blazes Larry is.

DAISY It's just anthrax, darlings. Only horses have anthrax. And
only Arabian mares die of it. (*to Fleece*) Isn't that right, darling?

MALLARD (*to Daisy*) You're wrong there. Why do you suppose
Larry keeps doping that scratch on his hand when he fools with it?

FLEECE (*quickly, yet her voice, manner, are cold, savage, as she
speaks to Larry*) Is that the truth? Have you got a scratch?

LARRY Maybe I'm already too full of poison to be susceptible to
anthrax.

FLEECE Or maybe you believe there really is a providence who
takes care of fools?

PELON Children, children. (*starts to pour the wine into the various cups*)

MALLARD That's right. Even if we have finished eating, let's think
about something a little more pleasant to talk about.

DAISY But even if Pelon catches it, Larry will just give him a squirt with his little needle—just as though Pelon were a horse, a stallion, himself—

THE GROUP (FAVORING DAISY)

DAISY *(to Pelon)* Then just think of the fun you'll have, galloping up and down the Range all day long, immune to anything any mare can do to you—

PELON *(calmly, pouring)* Then I must be already inoculated. I have been running this Range for twenty years already, and I haven't had any trouble yet avoiding what the Señora calls mares—

FLEECE *(to Daisy)* Aren't you a little wrong, yourself?

DAISY I can be. Am I?

ANOTHER ANGLE   (FAVORING FLEECE)

FLEECE *(as Larry holds her cup to be filled)* You don't inoculate to cure anthrax. You inoculate to prevent it. The inoculation itself gives you anthrax.

Larry turns his head suddenly, listening. He moves his cup slightly so that the pouring wine misses it.

PELON *(to Larry)* Watch it, Señor.

Larry looks back, moves cup back beneath the bottle, looks at Fleece again.

FLEECE *(continuing; to Daisy)* If you already have it, you may die. If you get an inoculation on top of it, you're probably sure to.

DAISY *(lightly)* Only, of course, another little squirt of the pure anthrax itself would be surer still.

LARRY *(to Fleece)* I don't guess that's some left-handed way of saying "Excuse me."

FLEECE *(to Larry; brief and cold)* If it was, it was an accident.

DAISY Well, nobody here has anthrax, so we don't have to worry.

FLEECE Worry about what?

DAISY *(airily, holds out her cup to Pelon)* About anybody dying from too much inoculation. If Larry hasn't got it already from that scratch, nobody here is in danger.

FLEECE *(to Daisy)* Did you think somebody was?

THE GROUP

LARRY Everybody is in danger. Look at the people every day that just want to cross the street for a bottle of beer or something.

PELON *(filling his flagon)* Look at us here. Two innocent harmless people who only wanted to marry each other. Three more innocent—

DAISY *(to Pelon; with mock grief)* What an insult! *(to all)* Is there no gentleman here?

PELON *(continues)*—and harmless people who only want to go to a horse show—

LARRY *(harsh and final as he puts an end to this)*—all snug and cozy, with a roof over us and plenty of firewood. *(prepares to get up)* So maybe we'd better settle down for the night while we're still warm.

DAISY Not until we've drunk the bride's and groom's health though. *(raises her cup)* That means only Pelon and Larry and me. You two can't drink it, darlings.

She looks at Larry, challenging. Pelon starts to raise his flagon, Larry makes a motion with his hand; Daisy and Pelon look down, pause. Daisy's expression does not change.

CLOSE SHOT   LARRY'S FLASHLIGHT DRINKING CUP

—overturned, beside his foot, the wine spilled.

LARRY'S VOICE Sorry.

Camera pulls back to include Pelon.

PELON I think it was my fault.

GROUP SHOT

Daisy with her cup still raised, her face smiling, yet rigid.

DAISY *(staring at Larry)* Fill it again.

LARRY *(gets to his feet)* Let it go.

DAISY *(smiling, staring at him)* Fill it again.

LARRY No. Consider it drunk. My best wishes to all, and to all, goodnight.

MALLARD *(moving to rise)* Larry's right. They've still got to improve on sleeping as a way to spend the night.

DISSOLVE TO:

INT. CABIN LATER

Daisy is just closing the lunchbox. The cloth is gone, the robe on which the meal had been spread is now folded aside. Daisy crosses room, sets the lunchbasket against the wall, where it bumps against Larry's bag. Daisy darts her hand quickly, as if she thought the bag was going to be overturned. But it remains upright. Daisy is looking at the bag with an expression which we register as the door is flung open and Pelon, followed by Mallard, snow on their feet and shoulders, etc., enter, each laden with an armful of pine and spruce boughs. Daisy returns. Mallard looks somewhat at a loss, but Pelon at once begins to spread the boughs on the floor, Daisy watching.

PELON *(spreading boughs)* I'm guilty. I was an Eagle Scout once.

DAISY Let this be a lesson to you, Rick. Always take a Boy Scout along when you elope to get married—

The door opens again. Larry enters, laden with boughs, approaches, drops them. But where Pelon was spreading them carefully, one by one, Larry scatters his load roughly with his foot. Daisy watches him.

DAISY You can see the difference now, Rick. Doctor Hanrahan was a wolf scout. He still is. Not the scout, of course.

LARRY Bring the robes.

Pelon takes up the folded robe. Mallard can help with this. They spread the robe on the boughs. Larry and Daisy both watch. Both of them seem to watch with a sort of contempt as Pelon and Mallard perform this womanlike chore.

DAISY Aren't they sweet?

Nobody answers. Larry lights a cigarette.

DAISY How are we going to sleep?

LARRY (*shakes out match; puffing*) I can't tell you. I learned when I was a child.

DAISY Maybe the bride should decide that. . . (*she stops, looks around*) Where is Toots? Weren't any of you responsible for her?

Larry, shaking the match, stops his hand in midair. Pelon and Mallard, half risen, look about. Suddenly Larry flings the match away, turns toward the door. Pelon and Mallard have not moved yet.

DAISY Maybe you'd better help him.

Pelon rises.

DAISY (*quickly; to Pelon*) Not you.

She is looking at Mallard now. Larry exits, shuts the door after him. Mallard rises slowly. Daisy watches him. He takes out a cigarette, his hands are trembling a little. Daisy watches him, then Pelon watches too.

DAISY Don't you even want her anymore, or is it just—?

PELON Señora— (*Daisy looks at him*) Will you kindly shut your blasted mouth—just for a little while?

DAISY (*vicious, furious, restrained*) It doesn't seem to have occurred to you yet that someday—

PELON (*interrupts*) I? I thought we had decided that I must have been inoculated for years.

He crosses rapidly to the door, exits. Daisy looks at Mallard, who is lighting a cigarette, his hands shaking.

DAISY Want me to light it for you?

MALLARD (*pauses, turns his head; after a moment*) Let's see your hand.

Daisy holds out her hand. Despite her, it begins to shake too, showing her own rage.

MALLARD Maybe we both need somebody to steady us.

DAISY I? I don't need anybody—or anything. See.

Before he can move, she snatches the match folder from him, strikes a match, holds it up.

CLOSE SHOT DAISY AND MALLARD

Daisy holding the match, which has burned almost down to her fingers, her hand steady as a rock now. Mallard watches, the flame touches her fingertips.

MALLARD Drop it!

She doesn't answer nor move, staring at the flame, her teeth bared, her face savage yet still. Just as the flame touches her fingertips, Mallard strikes her hand, knocking the match away.

EXT. CABIN LARRY (SNOW) NIGHT

—standing in snow. Before him in the snow is Fleece's trail. He looks grim, walks on, camera moving with him.

EXT. THE TRAIL LARRY

—has stopped again. There is something wrong with him. He appears to be dizzy, is fighting it off. It is not too apparent yet. When he takes the next step, stumbles, and falls to his hands and knees in the snow, it might still be normal. But as he remains so, his face raised, we see that he himself recognizes that something is wrong. Still kneeling, he raises a handful of snow, starts to rub it across his forehead as if to wake himself, seems to think better of it, drops the snow, gets to his feet, seems to pull himself together, so that he looks normal again when Fleece hurries in, stumbling in the snow.

EXT. TRAIL FLEECE AND LARRY (SNOW) NIGHT

FLEECE *(tense)* You fell.

LARRY *(himself now, so that even the effort he must be making is not discernible)* Where do you think you're going?

FLEECE I'm going to get out of here.

She stares at him. But he now hides whatever it is, looks as usual, grim and cold.

FLEECE   What is it? *(suddenly)* Let me see that scratch on your wrist.

She reaches for his wrist. He knocks her hand away before she can touch him.

LARRY   Not that I blame you. But you'll have to stick it out too.

FLEECE   You fool! Don't you know why I wanted to get away from there?

LARRY   Sure. But I can protect you from my girl friend—

FLEECE   I can protect myself from her. It's you.

LARRY   So that's why you were waiting for me. You take a lot of being eloped with, don't you? Twice in twelve hours—

FLEECE   Not anymore—at least not with a guy that can't stay on his feet. *(turns)* Come on. Let's get back to the cabin.

LARRY   *(turns; drily)* Yeah, so do I.

MOVING SHOT   LARRY AND FLEECE

—returning, as Pelon meets them and stops in the trail, facing them.

FLEECE   *(about to pass Pelon)* We changed our minds. Romeo fell down.

PELON   *(stares hard at Larry)* Fell down?

FLEECE   *(viciously, mimicking Larry, still trying to pass Pelon, who is still blocking the trail)* Yes, so do I.— We'll go back and give him a shot of anthrax serum; that'll pick him up.

LARRY   *(to Pelon)* Get out of the way. Let's get back inside the house.

PELON   *(blocking the trail, staring at Larry)* When we have already come this far? We will go on to the highway. The señorita can make it; she is better than most men—

Larry steps forward. Pelon puts out his hand quickly, but as quickly Larry half strikes, half pushes Pelon to one side.

LARRY   That's right. Show Miss Teller your knife too. *(to Fleece; shoving her on)* Go on.

They pass Pelon, go on. Now that no one can see it, Larry's face shows that something is wrong with him. Pelon follows, sober and thoughtful.

DISSOLVE TO:

INT. CABIN   DAISY AND MALLARD   (ANGLE TOWARD DOOR)

Daisy is standing quite near Mallard as Fleece, followed by Larry and Pelon, enters. Daisy apparently has just turned when she heard the door about to open; her hand is withdrawing as if she had been grasping Mallard's arm. Mallard glances up, then back toward the fire. He is smoking a cigarette. Daisy looks quickly from Fleece to Larry. There is a curious expression on her face. Her voice is silken, taunting.

DAISY   So soon? We're surprised. *(to Fleece)* Don't tell me it didn't take him any longer than this to get through finding you.

Fleece doesn't answer, goes on to the fire.

LARRY   Shut up, will you.

DAISY   *(watching Fleece)* Or maybe you're the one it was too cold for.

LARRY   Daisy. *(she stares at him, smiling and vicious)* This is another time it's lucky for you you're not a man.

DAISY   Very. But Rick's a man. Or maybe you don't think he is, either?

Larry looks at Mallard. Still smoking, Mallard looks up. They stare at each other.

LARRY   *(to Mallard)* Maybe you didn't hear. It's your fiancée she's talking about.

MALLARD   *(smoking)* Maybe I did hear.

LARRY   And maybe you play along with her, is that it?

MALLARD   So what?

ANOTHER ANGLE   (FAVORING LARRY AND MALLARD)

Larry slaps Mallard. Mallard sees the blow coming, raises his hand, but too late, as Larry slaps the cigarette into his face, mashing it, has Mallard off balance.

FLEECE   Stop it!

Larry swings his left. Mallard is still off-balance but manages to half-block, catching Larry's wrist and holding it for a moment.

CLOSE SHOT   LARRY AND MALLARD

Mallard, gripping Larry's wrist for a second; a queer expression comes over Mallard's face. He has felt Larry's fever. A second later, Larry jerks the wrist free. Mallard, having caught his balance, jumps back and free, his face still showing surprise and comprehension.

FLEECE   *(entering in background)* Rick! Stop it!— Pelon—

CLOSE SHOT   DAISY

—watching the two men, her eyes glittering, enjoying it.

THE GROUP

Larry, Mallard on guard now, looks about. He is out of his head a little, although only Fleece knows it and Mallard suspects it, as Pelon is about to do.

LARRY   *(to Fleece, coldly)* What's the matter? Look at Mrs. Otis' face. And what else do you expect? Maybe this is what you've been working for. We've got to pass the night someway. Okay, here it is. *(to Mallard)* Put your hands up.

MALLARD   *(on guard; glances quickly off)* Pelon—

LARRY   What? Hollering already? What'll you have left to do when you're really hit?

SHOT OF THE FIGHT   LARRY AND MALLARD   (THE OTHERS IN BACKGROUND)

Larry swings again. Mallard is pretty good with his fists. Larry in his present state of fever is wild, reckless, does not realize that Mallard is not fighting back. Mallard ties him up, holds both Larry's arms clenched. They struggle until suddenly Larry manages to hurl him off, flings him across the room until he brings up by slamming into the wall, still on his feet, Larry coming in again.

FLEECE Rick!

MALLARD *(quickly aside)* Sorry, Fleece. I'll have to knock him out—

LARRY *(coming in)* When you can—

They fight, as much of it as you want, to show Larry, actually not hit yet but so wild on his feet and in his swings that it is obvious something is wrong. Mallard, protecting himself, takes his chance, straightens Larry with a light left, hits with follow-up. Larry half-blocks the blow, it obviously does him no harm, yet he staggers slightly as if he had been hit. A dazed look on his face, he blunders into the wall, stands leaning against it, fights for return of senses, all watching him, amazed, since only Mallard and Fleece and Pelon know what had [happened] or is happening. He pulls himself together.

LARRY Sorry, Rick.

MALLARD It's all right.

Larry starts across the room. He is walking all right now, though all watch him, Daisy still glittering, Fleece anxious, Pelon watchful. He reaches the door.

LARRY And you, ladies—

He opens the door, passes out. Fleece starts suddenly after him.

MALLARD *(moves forward)* Wait—

PELON *(to Mallard)* No. I will.

Pelon exits.

INT. CABIN MALLARD, FLEECE, DAISY

MALLARD *(gently, to Fleece)* Come on to the fire. You're cold.

FLEECE *(obeys him)* He's got fever.

MALLARD I know. I felt his wrist.

Fleece doesn't answer, staring at Mallard.

DAISY *(idly)* Oh, that scratch on his wrist. The stallion disease.

Lucky it's not fatal . . . I'm cold, too. (*quickly, though Mallard has not moved*) No thanks, Rick. One patient is enough for you at a time. I'll help myself.

She crosses to where her coat hangs, just above and to one side of Larry's medical bag. She fumbles at it. The coat slips from her hand, falls, and for a moment half covers the bag. Daisy stoops, her body now hides the fallen coat and the bag; as she fumbles at the coat it seems to slip again and cover the bag completely, though almost at once she rises, the coat in her hand.

EXT. CABIN   LARRY AND PELON   (SNOW)   NIGHT

Larry standing in the snow. We cannot see what he is doing for a time, he is so still. Then he snaps his lighter on, takes something from his mouth, examines it by the lighter. We see it is a thermometer. He looks at it, begins to shake it as he turns, the lighter still burning. His hand stops the shaking, he stops, half-turned. A second, then he snaps out the lighter.

LARRY   (*quietly, turning*) That you, Pelon?

Pelon moves out from beside a tree.

LARRY   Got enough fresh air?

PELON   If you have.

LARRY   Okay. Let's go in.

They walk toward the cabin.

INT. CABIN   FULL SHOT

Daisy stands, leaning against one corner of the fireplace, easily and indolently, smoking, her left hand hanging close against her side, the hand hidden by her coat. Mallard stands at the other side of the fire. Fleece is kneeling, spreading the robe over the boughs as Larry and Pelon enter. Fleece looks up, at Larry, then at Pelon. Her face shows strain, anxiety, which she is keeping hidden, or at least smoothed over. Pelon's face tells nothing also.

FLEECE   (*rising*) Now we've had our fun. It's time we started doing what we're going to call sleeping—or at least getting the night passed.

LARRY We won't have to worry about that. The night'll attend to that, itself.

FLEECE Then let's give it a chance. *(to Larry)* You seem to have elected yourself boss here—driving the wood-carriers and herding back the runaways. You can start this too. Daisy and I'll take the outside—

DAISY *(yawning, indolent, not moving)* Only I doubt if I'll stay there. I usually don't. All to the contrary will so state now or forever after hold their peace—

FLEECE All right, all right. *(to Larry)* Come on. Break the ice.

Larry glances at the bed, but he crosses to one of the blocks of wood and pushes it with his foot over against the wall. The block starts to overturn. Fleece catches it, tilts it back up. All watch, Daisy lazily, as Larry sits down on the block.

LARRY Too early yet. We haven't hardly got started. Rick and I've got a fight to finish yet.

FLEECE *(loses control for the moment)* Don't you ever quit? Don't you ever give up?

LARRY *(easily)* Sure. Always quit. Hundred times a day, more or less. *(he looks about, finds Mallard)* What say, Rick—?

DAISY Larry's right. We haven't even begun it yet.

INT. CABIN THE GROUP (FAVORING DAISY)

—as she moves, stands away from chimney, smoking indolently and lazily, her left hand still down.

DAISY The wake, of course. Love died here tonight. Rick has lost his bride; Larry—

LARRY Sure. Always lose. Hundred times a day, more or less.

FLEECE *(to Daisy)* But you don't lose—never.

DAISY Me? I don't even put in the game. I'm the consolation prize. *(to Larry)* I can console, can't I, Larry? *(a little louder)* Larry. Don't go to sleep, darling.

Larry rises.

LARRY   Fleece is right. Let's get some rest. As soon as daylight comes, Rick and Pelon will have to start for the highway—

DAISY   *(watching him)* You aren't going?

LARRY   What? Yeah. *(to Mallard and Pelon, speaking distinctly as though instructing them)* We'll start at daylight—

MALLARD   Why not now? We can make it.

LARRY   No. Daylight will do. There won't be anything there now. But the plow and the highway gang will be through by daylight— the road will be open then—they'll have a car you can use for the girls—maybe they'll even send a tractor in here and dig one of our cars out. Daylight'll do. *(he looks from Mallard to Pelon)* At daylight.

MALLARD   Okay. We'll start at daylight.

LARRY   You can make it—

DAISY   *(watching him)* Not *we*, darling?

FLEECE   Now let's try to sleep. *(to Larry)* Come on. You're running this. Show us the way.

DAISY   *(moves, her left hand still down)* Then we should say good-night to him first.

FLEECE   All right. Say it.

DAISY   *(moves in to Larry, smiling, lazily and secretly)* But not so coldly. Of course, we have witnesses, but then won't we all? *(puts her right arm around Larry's neck)* Goodnight, darling.

FLEECE   It's late. Let's quit playing now.

DAISY   *(holding Larry with her right arm, looking at Fleece)* Aren't you a little previous? You don't begin to interfere with your husband's women until after the ceremony.

FLEECE   All right. Go on. Get it over.

LARRY   *(starts to push her away)* Cut it out, Daisy.

DAISY   Didn't you just hear her say get it over? *(draws him toward her)* Goodnight, darling.

Larry holds back another moment, glances about.

SHOT OF THE OTHERS

—watching

LARRY AND DAISY   MED. CLOSE SHOT

Larry's face shows annoyance.

   LARRY Okay.

He kisses her, very cold, platonic, is about to draw back when Daisy begins to kiss him. There is something like a struggle.

WIDER ANGLE   (TO INCLUDE THE OTHERS)

All watching, puzzled, until Fleece speaks.

   FLEECE Pelon!

Pelon starts forward. At this moment they break. Daisy stumbles back, staggering as Larry hurls her away and begins to strike at his right upper arm with his left hand.

CLOSEUP   LARRY'S RIGHT ARM

His big hypodermic needle, the one containing the pure anthrax, dangles from his arm, the needle buried in the flesh. Pelon's hand enters, strikes the needle out, it disappears. Fleece moves in.

CLOSE SHOT   DAISY

—as she watches, her teeth bared, her eyes glittering. She looks quickly up, reacts to surprise, alarm, starts to scream.

CLOSE SHOT   FLEECE

—as she swings the lunchbox down.

CLOSE SHOT   DAISY

—as she falls against wall, sinks to the floor, out. The lunchbox, flung by Fleece, crashes into the wall beside her.

GROUP SHOT   (DAISY NOT INCLUDED)

Fleece has just turned Larry's sleeve up above the puncture. Pelon holds the hypodermic, the plunger all the way in, Mallard near.

PELON   *(rapidly examines needle)* That was all of it.

MALLARD   *(to Pelon)* We'll start for the highway now. *(to Larry)* How much time will you—?

LARRY   Pinch yourself. It was just serum—not strychnine.

PELON   Who do you hope to comfort with that lie? It was the anthrax itself.

MALLARD   *(to Pelon)* Then come on.

FLEECE   No. I'll go. *(indicates corner where Daisy lies)* She won't stay out forever; don't you see, one of you will have to be here when she comes to. *(rapidly, tensely)* I can make it. Haven't I lived in these mountains for four years now? Do you think I never saw snow before?

LARRY   *(looking off)* So has Daisy.

All pause, look offscene.

CLOSE SHOT   DAISY   ON THE FLOOR

Her eyes are open now, though she has not quite collected her senses. Now her eyes regain vision; she comes completely to, staring at them.

LARRY'S VOICE   Help her up. *(after a moment)* Pelon.

Pelon enters, takes hold of her arm. She watches him, her eyes are watchful now. She is about to resist.

PELON   Get up. Nobody here's going to hurt you.

DAISY   Did anybody here think you were?

She gets up, Pelon helping her. As soon as she is up, she frees her arm.

DAISY   Thanks.

THE GROUP

Daisy touches her head, lightly, looks down, sees the lunchbox, looks at it, looks at Fleece.

DAISY   Thanks to everybody—for everything.

LARRY   Do you think you can make it out to the highway with Rick and Pelon?

DAISY   I'm leaving, am I?

FLEECE   Yes, you're leaving.

DAISY   Oh, yes, I'm leaving all right. *(to Mallard and Pelon)* It won't be a race, either. Do you think I'm afraid of you and your police?

FLEECE   No, I don't think you're afraid of anything. Not even of Daisy Otis. Just get out of here.

DAISY   Oh, another Hemingway character. Now we've got two of them. I'm going. *(she goes toward the door)*

LARRY   Wait.

Daisy doesn't stop.

LARRY   *(continues; to Mallard)* There's a pair of rubber boots in the station wagon. Get them for her.

MALLARD   Yes. Who do you want me to telephone?

LARRY   Call Professor Hoffmeyer at the University. Pelon knows.

MALLARD   *(putting on his overcoat which Pelon brings him)* Soon as the highway people are up, we'll come in with a tractor and get you out—we can leave word with them to send Hoffmeyer on as soon as he can get up the Pass—

LARRY   No. Get some grub and wait in the Pass for Hoffmeyer and bring him in with you. I don't think I'm going to be doing much moving in another hour.

FLEECE   *(to Pelon and Mallard)* Go on! Go on!

MALLARD   You ought to have more wood before we go—

FLEECE   Don't stop for firewood! Get on!

They exit. Fleece turns to Larry, sees that he has gone to the wall and has taken up his medicine bag.

MED. CLOSE   LARRY AND FLEECE

Larry, with the bag open on the block, has removed the vacuum bottle of serum, is now opening the hypo needle.

FLEECE   What are you going to do?

The door bursts open, Mallard enters.

INT. CABIN   MALLARD, LARRY, FLEECE

MALLARD   *(rapidly)* She got the boots herself and broke and ran. Pelon's trying to catch her, but I don't think he will— What are you doing?

LARRY   *(filling the needle from the bottle of serum)* It's okay. We know where she's going.

MALLARD   Yes, she can't go anywhere except back to the highway.

LARRY   *(filling needle)* I didn't mean that. She's running back to her husband.

MALLARD   But she said she wasn't afraid.

LARRY   *(busy with needle)* That's why she said it.

The door opens again. Pelon enters.

PELON   She's gone— *(sees what Larry is doing)* Ah. You have the serum—

FLEECE   *(cries)* The serum!

MED. CLOSE GROUP SHOT

The filled needle now lies on the block. Larry is turning back his sleeve.

MALLARD   The serum? You can't do that!

He reaches suddenly for the needle, as suddenly Fleece snatches it up.

FLEECE   *(fiercely)* Yes!

MALLARD   She's already given him pure anthrax; he says himself his serum doesn't always work. We'll have Hoffmeyer here tomorrow—

FLEECE   When somebody gets to the road and telephones him— yes!

MALLARD   *(to Larry)* No, you can't do it. We won't let you.

FLEECE   *(to Mallard)* When Larry and I both say yes?

MALLARD   *(to Fleece)* But Pelon and I say no. And we are stronger than you and Larry. *(turns)* Pelon—

ANOTHER ANGLE   (FAVORING PELON)

—as all watch him. His face is calm, unworried.

PELON   *(to Fleece)* Give him the needle, madonna.

CLOSE SHOT   LARRY AND FLEECE

The needle in his arm, as Fleece pushes the plunger home, removes the needle, flings it away.

FLEECE   *(to Larry)* Now will you quit? Will you give up now?

LARRY   Okay.

DISSOLVE TO:

EXT. CABIN   FLEECE   DAY JUST BREAKING

—with a tremendous armful of firewood, approaches cabin.

INT. CABIN   FLEECE   FAINT FIRELIGHT

—enters, carries the wood across and dumps it on a big pile which she has not only kept up but actually increased alone and singlehanded during her vigil, puts a few sticks on the fire until it blazes up, lights the room better. We can now see Larry's still shape in the bunk.

CLOSE SHOT   LARRY   IN BUNK

—asleep or in coma, carefully covered by the robe. Fleece enters, leans quietly over him a moment, touches his forehead to check on fever, turns and exits, going out again after more wood.

DISSOLVE TO:

EXT. MOUNTAINS   DAYBREAK

Pelon has stopped in the snow, exhausted, half resting against a tree. He shows the signs of his race through the snowy woods. Mallard enters, some distance back on the trail, struggles up, weary and spent too. Pelon doesn't look around when Mallard stops beside him.

MALLARD AND PELON   BY TREE

MALLARD   She beat us.

PELON   Yes. She's reached the highway by now. Don't talk to me about frail females, Señor. But then, she was born and raised in these mountains.

MALLARD   Even that shouldn't have made her a murderess.

PELON   It may cure her though.— Listen!

They listen. A faint sound comes from ahead.

PELON   It's the snowplow. They'll have a line crew along and maybe they will tap the wire for us and we can telephone for Hoffmeyer from the Pass. Come on.

They move on again, hurrying as fast as the snow will let them.

DISSOLVE TO:

EXT. HIGHWAY   IN THE PASS   SNOWPLOW   MORNING

—clearing snow from the road, snow whirling away as it butts forward. From ahead comes sound of an automobile horn, being tooted raucously and steadily. Other samples of activity are in view: highway trucks with sand, work trucks, telephone linemen trucks, police, unmarked coupes bearing only official tags belonging to superintendents, men in sight—crewmen, cops, mountaineers, etc.

EXT. ANOTHER PART OF HIGHWAY   A LINE OF STALLED CARS

—waiting for the road to be cleared. They have been here all night. The steady raucous blatting of the horn comes from somewhere in the line of them. A highway crewman or cop enters, looking for the car which is making the stupid noise. He pauses along the line, hunting for it, camera moving with him. First car contains a family of Okies, a battered Ford; then comes a milk or bread truck; then a costly limousine; then a jalopy, topless, painted up and covered with gadgets: spotlights, searchlights, three or four horns and klaxons, etc., and containing three teenage youths. They are not drunk. They are simply tired, sleepy, bored. They are blowing the horn. The cop makes them stop, or they stop when he comes up.

A YOUTH   *(to cop)* How much longer'll it be?

COP Not long—if you lay off that horn.

The cop goes on to the next car, containing an old couple.

COP You folks all right?

WOMAN Yes, officer. How much long—?

COP *(going on)* Not long now.

EXT. NEAR HIGHWAY   A CREW

—working around a tractor-scraper. The engine is running. Mallard and Pelon emerge from the forest and approach at the same weary gait, a sort of stumbling trot. The men around the tractor notice their snow-bedraggled garments and other signs of their long tramp through the snow.

FOREMAN Got off the road, huh?

PELON Yes. Have you seen a—?

MALLARD *(to Pelon)* Save it now. *(to foreman)* We're in a cabin about five miles up that old road there. We left a sick man in it. We've got to find a telephone and call a doctor. Is there a telephone line crew—?

FOREMAN Sure. About a quarter of a mile down the highway. *(he climbs into the tractor cab)* Jump on.

Mallard and Pelon get on the tractor. The rest of the crew swing aboard as the tractor starts moving.

DISSOLVE TO:

EXT. THE HIGHWAY   LATER THAT MORNING

It is almost cleared now. The snowplow can be heard in the distance, as it moves on. Other activities. In near foreground stands an official's coupe, bearing highway tag.

EXT. THE HIGHWAY   A TELEPHONE POLE   PELON, MALLARD,
THREE OR FOUR LINEMEN, HIGHWAY PEOPLE

—at the foot of the pole, a portable telephone set. Wires extending up the pole. Mallard talking into receiver.

MALLARD *(into telephone, tensely)* Professor Richard Hoffmeyer

. . . I know, he won't be awake yet. It's a matter of life and death—
I'm talking from the Pass, over the telephone company's emergency
set. . . Yes, I'll give you the message— Thanks. Tell him Doctor
Larry Hanrahan—H-a-n-r-a-h-a-n *(speaks slowly and distinctly
now, though still tensely)* has - had - an - accident - and - got - a - full
- hypodermic - into - his - arm. He will understand. We will be
waiting for him in the Pass. Got that? . . . Yes, thanks. *(he closes the
circuit)* Now I want to make a police call too. Is that okay?

A LINEMAN   There's a highway cop up ahead there.

MALLARD   How far?

PELON   *(looking out)* Look!

Mallard rises quickly. All look out.

EXT. NEAR HIGHWAY   DAISY   (FROM THEIR VIEWPOINT)

—has just appeared from concealment—highway gear or a clump of
bushes—and is running toward the parked official coupe. She was
apparently concealed near enough to have overheard, perhaps the
whole scene, but Mallard's reference to the police anyway.

EXT. HIGHWAY   BY TELEPHONE POLE   GROUP

—looking out of scene, surprised, as Pelon recovers first, starts to
run. After a moment Mallard follows.

EXT. HIGHWAY   THE COUPE   DAISY

—runs in, glances back, jerks the door open, gets in, bangs the door
shut, fumbles for switch. The engine starts, the gears grind, the
engine racing as the coupe leaps away.

EXT. HIGHWAY   A SHORT DISTANCE FROM TELEPHONE POLE
PELON AND MALLARD

Mallard has now gripped Pelon and is holding him back.

PELON   Let me go, Señor.

MALLARD   *(calmly)* Hold it. She's not going anywhere—just back
to her husband.

PELON   *(staring after car)* Sí—so Larry said. Maybe I was inoculated too soon, after all.

MALLARD I wouldn't want to know that one, anyway. Come on. Let's go back and find that cop. He can telephone down to the Junction, and they'll stop her there. *(Pelon turns, unwillingly)* Listen! Those other cars are beginning to move.

PELON *(stops, his face reacts to an idea)* Sí. I hear too. You go speak to the policeman. I'll wait for you here.

MALLARD *(goes on)* Okay.

He exits. Pelon turns toward the road, his face grim and expectant, determined.

GROUP   AT TELEPHONE POLE

The crew still waiting as Mallard enters.

MALLARD *(to foreman)* You said there was a cop—

FOREMAN Up ahead there with the highway Super. *(he turns; Mallard follows)* We'll take the service car.

MOVING SHOT   MALLARD AND FOREMAN

—walking.

FOREMAN What did the dame do?

MALLARD *(following)* She laid all her chips on the wrong color— or maybe the wrong wheel.

FULL SHOT   THE CARS

—as they begin to move, going down the mountain. The first one is the Oakie Ford, then the milk truck. Then with a blast of the raucous horn, the jalopy darts past the milk truck, still blatting the horn, and surges recklessly around the Okie Ford.

EXT. HIGHWAY   PELON

Sound of jalopy's horn as it approaches. Pelon steps quickly into the highway, the jalopy blats at him, but he holds his ground, so that the jalopy has to stop or else run him down. He approaches the driver.

DRIVER *(angrily)* Whataya tryin' to do—get run over?

PELON *(grimly)* No. Can you catch that car ahead?

DRIVER   Why do I wanta catch it?

PELON   *(with smart psychology)* No, I think you can't—not with this. I'd better find something which can run.

DRIVER   *(taking bait)* I can catch anything.

PELON   *(steps over side into back)* Good. Let me see you.

The jalopy starts on, blatting two or three different horns.

DAISY   IN THE STOLEN COUPE

—driving down mountain road. She is going fast, grim and now frightened: not sorry but just scared and determined. She swings the speeding car recklessly around curves.

                                        DISSOLVE TO:

SAME SCENE   LATER

Daisy has heard a sound behind her. She reacts to it as we distinguish what it is: the long wail of a police siren overtaking her. She presses down on the throttle.

INSERT: SPEEDOMETER   IN DAISY'S COUPE

The needle jumps to top speed.

                                        BACK TO:

DAISY'S CAR

It swerves, skidding around a curve, manages to hold.

CLOSEUP   DAISY'S FACE

—as it reacts, but still determined.

DAISY   IN COUPE

She looks over her shoulder, siren louder, looks back just in time to save the car from going off the road. Her face reacts as she fights the wheel. Siren louder. Her face shows horror, she flings up both hands before her face.

EXT. MOUNTAIN ROAD   CLOSE SHOT   DAISY'S CAR

—as it skids, leaves the road, tumbles down mountain side. The siren grows louder as it approaches.

CLOSE MOVING SHOT   THE JALOPY

—as it rushes down the mountain road, Pelon leaning forward in rear seat, the driver and his companion holding down the siren button as the siren wails. Pelon sees something offscene, reacts, leans over, cuts the switch.

PELON AND DRIVER   IN JALOPY   (PROCESS)

—struggling over the switch and hand-brake as jalopy slows.

    PELON   I will get out here.

CLOSE SHOT   JALOPY

—almost stopped, slow enough for Pelon to jump out. The jalopy straightens, gains speed, the siren wails again, continues to wail as the jalopy goes rapidly on.

CLOSE SHOT   PELON

—turns, his face sober and grave now.

                               DISSOLVE TO:

PELON   AT EDGE OF PRECIPICE

—with marks showing where something (Daisy's car of course) went over. Pelon enters. The jalopy siren has died away now, but as Pelon stops at the gap and looks down, the sound of another approaching siren begins, in a different key, also coming down the mountain. Pelon sees the wrecked car out of scene, reacts, crosses himself. The approaching siren is louder. He turns to face the sound.

PELON   BESIDE HIGHWAY

—waiting as a motorcycle policeman enters. Pelon's hand is raised until the policeman sees him, comes swiftly up, stops his machine, gets off.

    POLICEMAN   *(glances quickly about)* Where is it?

Then he too sees the marks where the car went over, advances quickly, Pelon following.

POLICEMAN AND PELON   IN THE GAP

—as the policeman looks down, sees the wreck out of scene, reacts. Pelon stands calmly beside him.

POLICEMAN   You were in that jalopy?

PELON   *(calmly)* Yes. I didn't know about the siren though.

POLICEMAN   *(grimly, looking down)* There's a name for this.

PELON   *(calmly)* Sí, Señor Capitan. It is called the hand of God.

POLICEMAN   *(starts down the cliff)* Better stick around.

PELON   I am not going anywhere.

FADE OUT.

FADE IN

INSERT: FRONT PAGE OF A NEWSPAPER

—held open in someone's hands. We see various headlines (boxes). Camera pans to one box and holds:

OTIS FUNERAL TODAY

Young Society Matron
Killed in Mountain Car
Wreck Last Saturday

Camera pulls back to show:

PELON   (SUNSHINE)   DAY

—standing beside the station wagon parked on the highway where the car jam was. Most of the snow is gone now, only a few traces here and there; traffic passing steadily on the highway beyond the station wagon, against the fender of which Pelon leans easily, the paper open in his hands as he reads it. Then, at sound of a car slowing offscene, he looks up, sees:

MALLARD'S COUPE

—as it stops facing the station wagon and Mallard gets out and approaches Pelon, his face anxious.

MALLARD   Hello. Didn't know whether you'd get my message or not.

MALLARD AND PELON   BY STATION WAGON

PELON   *(tranquilly)* We thought you'd be up today.

MALLARD *(anxiously)* What's the news?

PELON He still has anthrax—and he is still alive. *(he folds up the paper)* You have locked your car?

MALLARD Yes.

PELON Let's go then.

As he opens the station wagon door, we see a load of groceries, supplies.

MALLARD *(getting in)* I meant—

PELON *(interrupts, as he starts around the hood to get in too)* I know. She is not afraid either. *(he gets in, prepares to start the engine)* A man has to die, but nobody has to be afraid. And sometimes, if there are enough who are not afraid, he does not even have to die. *(he starts the engine)*

MALLARD Yes.

The car moves.

DISSOLVE TO:

EXT. THE CABIN   (SUNSHINE)   DAY

The snow has melted save for spots here and there. The scene looks like spring. The station wagon is parked before it.

The door opens. Fleece comes out, followed by Mallard. She looks worn-out, tense with strain, but not worried nor afraid. She comes out into the sunshine and stops, looking about, breathing the air which is like spring now. Mallard stops beside her.

MED. CLOSE TWO SHOT   MALLARD AND FLEECE

MALLARD He's got a lot against him. *(Fleece looks at him)* He's got me too.

FLEECE *(examines Mallard's face, her own face still serene)* Do you expect me to believe that?

MALLARD *(after a moment)* No. I guess it just wasn't on the wheel for me. No matter— *(he stops himself)*

WIDER ANGLE

While they look at each other, the cabin door opens and Hoffmeyer emerges. He is a slightly snuffy man of 50, carelessly dressed, yet practical and dependable looking as well as irascible and intelligent. Fleece and Mallard look back.

HOFFMEYER Didn't Pelon bring my beer? If he didn't, he can turn right around and go back for it—

FLEECE He just took it into the house, Doctor.

HOFFMEYER He'd better have.

He glares a moment, then reenters the cabin.

CLOSER SHOT   THE TWO

FLEECE (*still serene, completing his unfinished sentence*) —no matter which way it goes? It's not going but one way.

MALLARD That's right. Doctors can be wrong. Even Hoffmeyer.

FLEECE (*serenely*) He will be this time. (*soberly*) I'm sorry, Rick.

MALLARD Forget it. I'm a gambler. I always bank the house. Only . . . maybe I just never gave odds like this before. (*he rouses*) Well, if you'll call Pelon to drive me back to the highway—

FLEECE Yes.

But she doesn't move yet, only watching him until he feels the look, looks at her, after a moment takes her by the elbows and is kissing her as Pelon enters in background.

MALLARD (*releases her*) Keep the head up, soldier.

PELON It is up, Señor. I told you that down at the road.

He enters, carrying the folded paper, hands it to Fleece.

PELON The latest horse-breeders' news.

She takes the paper, scarcely hearing him. Pelon turns to Mallard.

PELON If you're ready . . .

MALLARD Right.

He follows Pelon out.

WIDER ANGLE   (TO INCLUDE STATION WAGON)

Fleece stands looking out of scene, watching, Sound of station wagon as Pelon starts it. Fleece raises the folded paper, watches at the sound of station wagon as it starts and pulls away. Then she lowers the paper, starts to turn, glances at the paper as though by chance, something catches her eye, she pauses, stops, begins to read.

INSERT: NEWSPAPER BOX

        ALL-WESTERN BROOD MARE
        SHOW DEFERRED UNTIL NEXT
        WEEK BECAUSE OF SNOWSTORM

        One of the favorites to win
        this ten thousand dollar prize
        is Lady Rea II, bred by Doctor
        Laurence Hanrahan but now owned
        by Miss Fleece Teller.

                            LAP DISSOLVE TO:

INSERT: NEWSPAPER BOX

        NEW ANTHRAX SERUM SAVES
        DISCOVERER'S LIFE

        Doctor Laurence Hanrahan
        . . . .

                            LAP DISSOLVE TO:

INSERT: NEWSPAPER BOX

        LADY REA II WINS ALL-
        WESTERN BROOD MARE PRIZE

                            LAP DISSOLVE TO:

EXT. SHOW GROUNDS   CLOSE SHOT   LADY REA II

—as the judges give the prize, applause from crowd, etc.

                            LAP DISSOLVE TO:

EXT. STALLION ROAD RANCH HOUSE   (SUNSHINE)   DAY
LADY REA II   FLEECE

—riding, coming at a good pace around the house, following the drive toward the stables.

EXT. AT STABLES

Larry, dressed, lying in the sun in a desk chair. Hoffmeyer beside him. Pelon is superintending while a stableboy grooms a horse. All look out of scene at sound of Lady Rea's feet as Fleece enters. Before she can stop hardly, Hoffmeyer is shouting at her.

HOFFMEYER I thought I told you to stay away from here! He is a sick man yet.

LARRY *(to Hoffmeyer)* Why didn't you tell her that up there at the cabin two weeks ago?

HOFFMEYER You were sick then—

LARRY *(rising)* I thought you just said I am sick now. *(he approaches Fleece)*

HOFFMEYER Larry! Come back here—

CLOSE SHOT HOFFMEYER (PELON BESIDE HIM)

Hoffmeyer is staring angrily out as Pelon appears beside him with an opened bottle of beer.

PELON Señor Doctor—

HOFFMEYER What?

He glances at Pelon, sees the bottle. A take, then he takes the bottle.

HOFFMEYER Thanks.

He starts to drink, starts to fire up again as he looks out of scene toward Fleece and Larry. Pelon nudges his elbow gently, so that the bottle seems to approach his mouth of its own accord. Hoffmeyer simmers down again, starts to drink. Pelon nudges Hoffmeyer's elbow again, so slightly and skillfully that the bottle seems to move of its own accord, until in order to put his lips to the bottle and drink, Hoffmeyer will have to turn his back to Fleece and Larry. This is what Pelon has been trying to do, to give Larry and Fleece some privacy in their scene. Hoffmeyer realizes this is what Pelon is doing, gives

Pelon a knowing look, turns his back squarely to Larry and Fleece, raises the bottle and drinks.

CLOSE SHOT   LARRY BESIDE FLEECE

—who still sits the horse.

FLEECE   I brought her back. I can't take her.

LARRY   You already have.

FLEECE   No.

LARRY   So I've got to marry you to make an honest horsewoman out of you.

FLEECE   No.

LARRY   That's right. I've just got to marry you—period.

FLEECE   No.

LARRY   (*draws her face down toward his*) Yes.

FLEECE   (*leaning down*) No.

LARRY   (*drawing her down, their mouths are about to meet*) Come on. Say it.

FLEECE   Yes.

FADE OUT.

THE END